THE WORLD'S GREATEST MYSTERIES

Investigating Our World's Most Fascinating
Secrets And Unsolved Mysteries

Bill O'Neill

ISBN: 978-1-64845-119-5

CONTENTS

Introduction 1

Pyramids: Alien Constructions or the Product of Slavery? 4

"I Come From Over the Way" 10

It's Neither Here nor There 16

There's Being a Peeping Tom, Then There's This!........................22

Two Little Shreks! 29

Did Anyone Bring a Map?..35

Useless or Important?..42

Hold the Lead Tightly!...49

One-Way Ticket to Wealth and Prosperity, Please!........................57

But What About the Poor Horse? 67

The Impossible Star 73

The True Identity of Jack the Ripper 78

WANTED: Any Information, At All, Please!................................88

Random Explosion or Mutant Sharks? 96

Does Anyone Have a Shovel?..103

The Two Princes' Disappearance....................................108

It's All Gone a Bit *Blair Witch* 113

"I Swear, I Left Them Right Here!" 119

Help! I've Knocked His Head Off!....................................125

The Housing Association From Hell 133

Conclusion..140

DON'T FORGET YOUR FREE BOOK

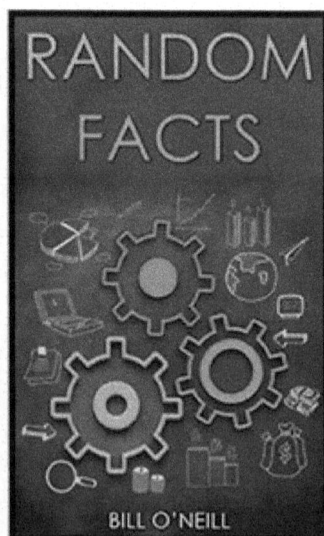

INTRODUCTION

"We are the middle children of history. Born too late to explore Earth, born too early to explore space." – An anonymous person on the internet.

If you ever explained to a philosopher from 16th century Italy that one day, people would walk the Earth with a small box that can access almost every known fact and myth ever conceived, they would either have you burnt at the stake as a heretic or hailed as a prophet.

We exist in a time of immense knowledge, built on 200 years of almost constant progress and advancement.

At this moment in time, you can read Wikipedia and become better informed within 20 seconds, you can access any major media outlet online, and you can observe countless hours of documentaries on the most important moments in human history. Such is the power of the internet.

What do most of us do with it, however? Look at conspiracy videos on TikTok and rewatch *Breaking Bad*.

We're at the end of humanity's big period of discovery. The world is largely documented save for the ocean, and you must be extremely clever to be involved with journeying there (which rules you out, of course).

Space is there to be conquered one day, but we're a long way from managing to do that. So, for now, the colossal amount of information, facts, knowledge, and past achievement has left us with, is very little mystery.

As a species, there's very little that's *mysterious* about the world now. Many modern-day mysteries are conspiracy theories about the royal family being lizards, or that becoming a United States president in the 21st century makes you immortal. They aren't mysteries: they're made-up theories because people want to *not* know something.

It's nice not to have an ending sometimes, it's good to leave things up to our imagination. Human beings with good imaginations survived longer when we were living out of caves and said "Ugg."

If the little caveman imagines that there's a big scary saber-toothed tiger mere feet from his home, then he doesn't go outside that night and stays indoors to be safe. Whereas the moron who lives next door to him doesn't think about that, and instead waddles outside to find himself being prepared as a light supper.

However, do not despair. There is a mystery out there, you just must find it. Not all tales and stories from our time on this Earth have a definitive answer that we know about. Crimes are left unsolved (less than 50% of homicides are solved in the USA, which is depressing), CCTV footage goes missing, years roll by, and we're left with a story or physical *thing* that doesn't seem to give us any real answers.

In this book, you will find a fantastical and fascinating (and sometimes funny) retelling of some of the greatest and weirdest mysteries ever. Some stories take place hundreds of years ago, some are far more recent, but all are without a confirmed ending to their story.

Here you will read about mysterious people who came from lands unknown, text written in unknown languages, unsolved murders, the unknowable cosmos, and much more. The book can be tackled in one go, if you like to turn your brain into a kind of chunky soup, or it can be attacked one bit at a time, to preserve your sanity.

Along the way, you're going to learn an abundance of interesting facts, but that's what comes from reading a book written by someone so exceptionally clever.

You won't be left alone to fill in the blanks, you will be led by the hand like a toddler going to the grocery store for the first time, or like a chimpanzee to a jar of peanut butter.

The most important thing of all is to enjoy yourself, learn what you can, and use it to baffle people at dinner parties.

Many of us simply need an *in*, and there are not many ins better than excitedly telling people about a bridge in Scotland that makes dogs kill themselves. It'll ruin the starter, but you'll be the most interesting person in the room.

For now, relax and enjoy the *World's Greatest Mysteries*, soon to be available in a brain near you.

PYRAMIDS: ALIEN CONSTRUCTIONS OR THE PRODUCT OF SLAVERY?

Seeing the Pyramids is a guaranteed feature on many people's bucket lists, alongside swimming with dolphins, and kicking a politician.

The triumphant peaks of the great pyramids of Egypt are usually the first that come to mind, but many types of pyramids appear across the world. These range from the Nubian pyramids in Sudan, constructed 1,000 years after the Egyptians, to the South American pyramids built by the Mayans and other civilizations.

Ultimately, pyramids are simply mysterious buildings. Archaeologists have used all available research to come to certain conclusions about them, but we must be careful.

Pyramids are one of the defining and most valuable ancient artefacts available to us and are fragile. Exploring carelessly could lead to long-lasting damage and we could lose some of the most important aspects of human history. Because of this, we haven't been able to investigate every aspect of the pyramids - so, the pyramids of Egypt have several great mysteries that are yet to be unsolved.

Mystery I: How on Earth did they do it?

It seems that humankind isn't entirely sure how the pyramids were built. The largest Egyptian pyramid, the Pyramid of Khufu, is made up of approximately 2.3 million individual stone blocks, each weighing anywhere from 2.5 to 16 tons.

More to the point, some of the stone used in the inner chambers comes from a region called Aswan, some 500 miles from Giza, where the pyramid is situated.

So, how did the Ancient Egyptians construct such colossal monuments to the dead, using blocks that no one person could lift, thousands of years ago?

Archaeologists have theories about how the stones got there, of course. One such concept is evidenced in a painting in the tomb of Djehutihotep, which shows blocks being moved using wet sand and a sloping landscape.

This very well may be the answer to how they got the stone there. It'd have been tough work, but the Ancient Egyptians weren't ever too worried about overworking their slave workforce. In actual fact the majority of workers were free men not slaves.

The big question to be asked then is how they managed to move the stone into position to form gigantic pyramids that are still standing thousands of years later.

There was none of the machinery currently in use like cranes that make the job easier in the 21st century, in fact. they only had the power of human beings and a few relatively rudimentary tools. And if we've learned anything from observing roadworks on the freeway, we know that having lots of people doesn't necessarily guarantee fast results.

Ramps have been found near pyramid sites, which provide some of the answers to this mystery, but it's still difficult to imagine how 15 tons of stone could be hauled up a steep ramp and then put into place. The theories continue to build and there's been no confirmed answer yet. However, most archaeologists agree that it wasn't an advanced alien race. Just don't ask the guy at the bar who promises to tell you all about it in exchange for a couple of Coors.

Mystery II: Who built them?

"Egyptians you idiot!"

Well, yes, but *which* Egyptians? For a very long time, it was assumed that enslaved workers built the pyramids.

During the pyramid's construction, thousands of unskilled slaves would have died due to falling stone, heat exposure, and exhaustion as they toiled to create what would become the world's greatest treasures from the ancient age.

The Ancient Greek historian Herodotus was the first to write about slaves as the great builders of the pyramids, which was in turn propagated by movies about Ancient Egypt, depicting the exploitation of thousands of unfortunate slaves.

However, in 1990, some graves were found that may well dispute that view.

The graves were uncovered near the Giza pyramids and stretched to approximately 9 feet deep. Inside the graves were the skeletal remains of 4,000-year-old pyramid builders, as in *paid* professional laborers.

The finding was hailed in 1990 as one with colossal ramifications. If we know for a fact that there were professionals building the pyramids, then perhaps the whole idea of slaves is incorrect.

Unfortunately, neither idea is true; both are merely theories at this stage. The whole "slaves" argument still prevails for many, while the technical know-how required to construct the huge monuments points some toward a highly skilled team of expert laborers being responsible.

Mystery III: Did it have a cherry on top?

The most magnificent of the Egyptian Pyramids is the Great Pyramid at Giza, standing at 454 feet with an overall volume of some 92 million cubic feet. It's a sight to behold even after seeing it in every pyramid-related documentary and piece of hotel art, and on every dodgy postcard.

However, if you go to the top of the vast monument, you'll be able to walk on it; in fact, you'd have more than 30 feet of space to walk around in. Which begs the question, why is it flat and not pointed?

The mathematical shape of a "pyramid" is a three-dimensional shape where points join at the top, in what is called the apex.

The Great Pyramid of Giza seems like a normal square-based pyramid with triangular walls, but there is no apex. However, many think that at some time there was. In fact, the Egyptian tourist board will tell you that sometime in the last few thousand years or so, thieves made off with what once adorned the top, the capstone.

This capstone has a lot of mystery about it, with no one able to completely confirm what it looks like. However, most archaeologists and amateur Egyptologists will tell you that it is essentially a small pyramid itself, which rested upon the top of the Great Pyramid of Giza and completed the pyramid shape. According to tradition, the capstone was added to complete the structure and give it its purpose.

Since the time of Jesus Christ, there have been writings about the missing capstone, with the ancient people confused as to why there would be this structure without its crown.

Many believe that the capstone would have been made entirely of gold, or at least covered with a layer of gold. With the pyramids themselves being made from polished limestone, the whole structure would have shone in the night, like a star that has fallen to Earth. It might have been visible from space…, if it ever existed.

What happened to the capstone remains a mystery. We have other capstones from the Ancient Egyptians but not one from the Great Pyramid at Giza. So where did it go? Because it's not easy to conceal a gigantic capstone made from or covered in gold, and it's even more difficult to sell one! Trust me, I've tried.

"I COME FROM OVER THE WAY"

Imagine yourself as a quite normal German soldier, stationed in Nuremberg (Germany, obviously) in 1828. The industrial revolution is just picking up speed and the world is changing at an amazingly fast pace. Societal structures are breaking down, with others replacing them, Europe is seemingly forever at war, and the world is changing its opinions on that whole colonization and slavery business that made much of Europe so rich. It's a confusing time. Even more so when you are presented with a letter, handed to you by a teenage boy, which reads:

"Von der Bäierischen Gränz daß Orte ist unbenant. 1828"

Unfortunately for us, you're not a German soldier from 1828, you're whoever you are, which means you likely don't know what that bit of text says. It's not because you're stupid, necessarily, it's just statistically likely that you don't know how to read German. The text says:

"From the Bavarian border, the place is unnamed. 1828"

Bavaria is a region of Germany, and the boy's note seems to say that he is from an unnamed location near its border and the year is 1828. The letter goes on further - I won't write it all in German because that would be more fruitless than a burned orchard - but here are the basic details:

- The writer, whoever that is, says that the boy holding the note was given to him on October 7, 1812, as an infant.
- The writer went on to educate the boy in how to read and write, and how to be a good Christian.
- The writer never let the boy out of his house.
- The writer acknowledges that the boy would now like to be a soldier and it is up to the captain as to whether he

11

takes him in or hangs him, either way is fine by the writer.

The teenager also possesses another letter, from his mother. She goes into further detail about the boy's father and even names the lad as Kasper Hauser, finally providing some real information that might help. The only problem is that both letters are written in the same handwriting and were probably just written by the boy.

Hauser was quickly imprisoned by the authorities as a "vagabond," a homeless person, which was a crime at the time. However, the story of the mysterious boy who knew a few prayers and could speak English to an acceptable standard spread quickly through Nuremberg. Hauser stayed imprisoned for two months and seemed to do well. He was physically in decent condition and intelligent enough to get by, though he refused all food and drink apart from bread and water.

The town and authorities were nonplussed. Who was this mysterious boy who had simply turned up one day? His story seemed spurious, yet here he was. Most assumed he was a half-wild child, who had been running amok in some nearby woods or forest, with only remnants of his memory working, providing him with a merely passable education.

After the two months' imprisonment, Hauser divulged to the mayor where he had come from, which only provoked more questions.

Hauser claimed that he had spent his whole life in solitary confinement, living in a dark cell. He estimated that the cell was about 6.5 feet long, 3.2 feet wide, and 4.9 feet high. There was a straw bed to sleep on, a few toys, two wooden horses, and a wooden dog.

Each morning Hauser woke to find bread and water next to his bed. Sometimes the water would taste bitter and make him drowsy, leading many to think he was being drugged. Hauser then said that one day, he met a man who taught him how to write his name and walk normally.

After he could do both, the man (who hadn't shown his face to Hauser) dropped him at Nuremberg and disappeared.

The story was the hottest gossip since Klaus had drunk too much at Oktoberfest and spread quickly. International attention came Hauser's way, with media from across Europe desperate to hear more.

Rumors abound as to who this strange person was. The more excitable were confident that he was an illegitimate prince, banished by the royal family following his imprisonment, while others claimed that he was merely an imposter, looking for a free handout from the government. Either way, Hauser continued to live in Nuremberg and remained a subject of interest.

The good people of Nuremberg raised money to enable Hauser to be adopted by the city, and he became quite popular. It was discovered that the young boy was good at drawing. He was placed in the care of schoolmaster and philosopher Friedrich Daumer, who liked to experiment on the boy to see how medicines and magnets reacted with him. Supposedly, the magnets had a peculiar interaction with Hauser, but this probably doesn't mean anything.

The rest of his story is filled with bizarre interactions with people. In 1829, the lad claimed to have been attacked at his home by a hooded man whom he recognized as the individual who had brought him to Nuremberg in the first instance. Hauser was cut across the forehead and left a trail of blood through his premises. The police intervened but found no suspects, though they moved him to the care of Johann Biberbach, a local authority.

While at Biberbach's place of residence, a pistol shot went off in Hauser's room. He was found with a head wound, and he claimed to have accidentally knocked the pistol while reaching for books. His story seemed doubtful and far-fetched, with many sure that he had been attacked by Biberbach for lying or fabricating his story. It was decided that Hauser's now strained relationship with Biberbach (after only a couple of months) meant he should be moved to live with Baron von Tucher. The latter would go on to tire of Hauser, accusing him of lies and vanity.

For the rest of Hauser's life, he never found permanent residence. Many figures were interested in taking him in, including other German authority figures as well as Lord Stanhope from England.

They all wanted to solve his bizarre mystery and unravel his tale. However, all became frustrated with the simple lad and found his answers to be suspicious and irritatingly vague. By December 1833, Hauser had argued with everyone who took an interest in him, and all of them had written that he was a scoundrel and would cheat anyone whom he could.

On December 14, 1833, Hauser suffered a deep wound in his chest. He told a tale of being attacked by a stranger with a knife, and a note was later found by a policeman. The note was written in reverse, like looking at it through a mirror. It read:

"Hauser will be able to tell you quite precisely how I look and from where I am. To save Hauser the effort, I want to tell you myself from where I come _ _ . I come from from _ _ _ the Bavarian border _ _ On the river _ _ _ _ _ I will even tell you the name: M. L. Ö."

Kasper Hauser died of his injuries on December 17, and the "killer" was never found, with many assuming that he'd given himself the injury.

The story is baffling. Who on earth was this person? He was either a member of royalty, a fraudster, a simpleton, a traumatized child, or quite simply unwell.

Either way, there isn't a definite answer. Hauser's tale was well documented by all who met him, with some insisting he was a criminal liar, but we're unlikely to ever find out exactly who Kasper Hauser was - or whether he was indeed even called Kasper Hauser!

IT'S NEITHER
HERE NOR THERE

Galileo Galilei was a fantastic astronomer who, in the early 17th century, disproved centuries-old theories in science and religion, and proved that there was more to the universe than meets the eye. His name was also used to brilliant effect in the song *Bohemian Rhapsody* by Queen, which is where most people know him from:

GALILEOOOO
GALILEOOOO
GALILEOO MAGNIFICOO-OH-OH-OOOHH

I'm just a poor boy nobody loves me... **HE'S JUST A POOR BOY FROM A -** you get the idea.

The prevailing thought in the 17th century was that the Earth (that's the planet we're on, by the way) was the center of the universe, and all things spin around us. It was also thought that there wasn't much more beyond what we could see: the loads of stars and the few planets that make up our solar system, which are sometimes visible to the naked eye.

Galileo improved the telescope and gazed into the abyss with more detail than anyone had ever done before. And what he found was that they were *wrong*.

Galileo saw hundreds of stars, far more than we can see with the naked eye. He saw the satellites of Jupiter and gazed upon the expanding universe. He found that we aren't in the middle of the universe at all. In fact, we're just one very, *very* small speck in it.

Moving forward to more modern scientific and astronomical observations, it was thought for decades of modern science that the universe is:

a) Expanding very quickly and has been since the dawn of time, but
b) Gravity will slow the expansion of the universe.

By the turn of the 21st century, it was thrown into question after the Hubble Space Telescope observed something unexpected in 1998.

The Hubble Space Telescope is a large telescope that sits in a low orbit around Earth and is seen as a vital piece of technology when it comes to the exploration and investigation of space.

From orbit, the telescope can better observe the cosmos more than our telescopes here on Earth, and in 1998, it observed that a very long time ago, the universe was expanding at a slightly slower rate than it was in 1998.

This means that gravity is not slowing down the expansion of the universe as Einstein's work would predict, and the universe's expansion is instead speeding up.

Here's where this gets mysterious. NASA scientists aren't 100% sure as to why the universe is expanding, but it does have a name: **dark energy**.

Not a great deal is known about dark energy. Scientists have figured out how much dark energy there is, through some very clever mathematics and understanding how it affects the universe's expansion.

It turns out that 68% of the universe is made up of dark energy, which is a spectacularly important thing to discover. However, *what* dark energy is - completely eludes our world's greatest minds. With most of the universe being dark energy, it's also been calculated that dark matter makes up a further 27%, which leaves less than 5% for the rest of the universe.

That encompasses everything that we can see or have detected with our instruments and then all detectable and knowable matter beyond that.

Just 5%.

This mystery isn't limited to human history: It's the greatest mystery of the universe. *What is it?* Sean Carroll, a cosmologist from the California Institute of Technology said, "we have a complete inventory of the universe…, and it makes no sense." So, let's have a look at some of the theories and big-brain thoughts about what dark matter and dark energy could be. Who knows, we might even unravel it all on this very page! (Unfortunately, we're not going to, sorry.)

Dark matter

In the 1970s, there was a broad agreement that the universe has more to it than it first seems. Scientists were working on the assumption that all matter (which is a 'word' used for stuff) gives off light and is observable. No one has ever said that this had to be the case, it was just assumed that that was the case. It was not until computer simulations were run about our galaxy, the solar system, that the simulation showed the disintegration of our entire galaxy.

Planets and stars were not held in by the center as there was not enough mass in the galaxy to hold it all together. So why are we not zooming away from our sun, with all our drinks being permanently transformed into a slushie?

There is lots of matter, far more than we can see. The galaxies all contain matter called 'dark matter,' some sort of invisible mass that doesn't radiate light. Discovering that dark matter exists was a huge discovery and dominated the rest of the 20th century's developments in the study of the cosmos. However, we still have no idea what the stuff is, we just know there's tons of it. It's confusing and slightly scary but knowing that dark matter exists has enabled us to understand that the universe is expanding and all because of another mysterious energy that seems like it might be stronger than gravity.

Dark energy

All we know of dark energy is that it's responsible for the acceleration of the expansion of the universe. It seems to be stronger than gravity and the fact that it exists poses infinitely more questions than answers. There are a few possibilities being investigated by scientists at the South Pole and space organizations across the world, with two being the most plausible:

1. Much of what Einstein said about gravity, which has underpinned all our knowledge and understanding of space, is either wrong or a little bit wrong.
2. Dark energy might be the energy that a vacuum creates. It might not be that, but inside the vacuum of space is certainly where it *is*. If this is true, it is the constant energy of the universe and is over 14 billion years old.

Either way, we don't know.

This story might be a little frustrating to read because there's no way that you can come up with an answer unless you have knowledge from another 50 years in the future. Even then, you may not have the answer! There's nothing more mysterious than the vast expanse of the universe, not even the continued success of Flo Rida is as mysterious.

THERE'S BEING A PEEPING TOM, THEN THERE'S THIS!

What's your place of residence known for? Some towns can boast an invention or two, others are proud of their famous residents.

For many smaller cities and towns, where people go about their lives quite happily and not much excitement tends to occur, the defining characteristic becomes an event. This is the case for Circleville, Ohio, a small city with a population of just under 14,000 as of 2020.

In 1976, several residents of Circleville received letters postmarked Columbus, Ohio. The letters detailed secrets and gossip about their lives, often their sex lives, and threatened to divulge their secrets to their community.

I'm not sure how you'd react to a letter divulging some of your juicier secrets. Perhaps dismiss it as a scam? Panic? Shout into the night "You'll not take me alive…!" Perhaps a sprint into the wilderness?

One of the very first residents to receive letters, Mary Gillispie, remained quite calm. Gillispie was a school bus driver and was accused repeatedly (via mysterious letters) of having an affair with Superintendent Gordon Massie. One of the more famous letters to Gillispie reads:

STAY AWAY FROM MASSIE:
DON'T LIE WHEN QUESTIONED OVER KNOWING HIM.
I KNOW WHERE YOU LIVE: I'VE BEEN OBSERVING
YOUR HOUSE AND KNOW YOU HAVE CHILDREN.
THIS IS NO JOKE: PLEASE TAKE IT SERIOUS.
EVERYONE CONCERNED HAS BEEN NOTIFIED
AND EVERYTHING WILL BE OVER SOON.

A chilling letter to receive, admittedly with a grammar error on line five. One can take something serious*ly*. Taking it "serious" doesn't make much sense, so don't let anyone tell you that this book won't teach you anything!

This story has just made you a better writer and will prevent you from getting into a silly argument on Facebook.

Back to the story. Gillispie simply denied that there was any such liaison happening with the superintendent. Her husband, Ron, may have been suspicious initially or simply trusted his wife, but things began to move more quickly when he received letters of his own.

Ron Gillispie's letters were more urgent. Ron was told to stop his wife from having an affair with Superintendent Massie immediately, otherwise the whole neighborhood would be informed, leading to public embarrassment for him and his wife. Just how did the writer want Mr. Gillispie to end the affair?

> *MR. GILLISPIE, YOUR WIFE IS SEEING GORDON*
> *MASSIE.*
> *YOU SHOULD CATCH THEM TOGETHER AND KILL*
> *THEM BOTH*
> *HE DOESN'T DESERVE TO LIVE.*

Ron Gillispie received further letters throughout the summer of 1977, threatening him with public exposure via billboards and posters. Mary and Ron brought in help from family in the shape of Ron's sister and husband Karen and Paul Freshour.

Between them, they decided that Paul would write a letter to a man called David Longberry, who had long had an infatuation with Mary Gillispie and was a fellow bus driver. Are you keeping up?

Well, Paul wrote a threatening letter of his own to David and the couple were left alone. It seemed that it *was* David all along and he had been frightened into stopping by Paul's involvement. That is until the evening of August 19 when Ron received a phone call at his house and flew into a rage. He grabbed his gun and said that he was going out to talk to the letter writer.

Only a few hours later, Ron was found dead at the site of a car crash, his truck having smashed into a tree. His gun had been fired at least once. The police had Ron's death down as dying as a result of drink driving, though his family were sure that the usually drink-wary Ron hadn't been drinking that day at all and doubted the police's finding.

More letters circulated around Circleville that alleged the local police were involved in covering up the murder of Ron Gillispie. As a result, the police released statements detailing their findings at the scene of Ron Gillispie's death and made mention of 'another party' who was never named.

It turns out Mary *was* having an affair with the superintendent, by the way, though she claimed this didn't start until after the letters arrived.

The letters continued into the 1980s and almost took another life in 1983. The mysterious Circleville writer had taken to placing signs up around Circleville alleging cover-ups and crimes that the citizens were committing.

Mary Gillispie remained a favorite of the writer and many posters were placed on her bus route accusing Superintendent Massie of sexual assault. While driving her bus, Mary became enraged and tore down one of the posters, almost losing her life in the process.

The poster had been rigged with a gun that would shoot at anyone who attempted to disturb the poster. Police investigated and found the gun to be registered to Paul Freshour, Ron's sister's husband. Paul maintained that his gun had been stolen, but as it hadn't been reported stolen, the police weren't interested.

Paul's handwriting was matched to the letters after he was asked to deliberately emulate the style of capitalized characters on the letter. The then-divorced Paul was sentenced to prison for attempted murder and for the harassment of the people of Circleville.

Let's pause and recalibrate for a moment:

- For approximately six years, the residents of Circleville, Ohio had been receiving threatening letters almost constantly.
- The Gillespie's had been particular targets of the writer.
- Ron Gillispie died in a suspicious car accident moments after receiving a phone call that made him very angry.
- His wife Mary was almost shot a few years later by the writer.
- Ron's brother-in-law has been connected to the crimes, given some dodgy tests that wouldn't stand up in any modern court of law, and sentenced to prison.

You don't need me to tell you that the letters didn't stop there. Even Paul received a letter while in prison:

NOW WHEN ARE YOU GOING TO BELIEVE YOU AREN'T GETTING OUT OF THERE?

I TOLD YOU TWO YEARS AGO.

WHEN WE SET 'EM UP, THEY STAY UP. DON'T YOU LISTEN AT ALL?

Paul regularly received taunting letters, sometimes while he was in solitary confinement with no access to the mail at all. After ten years in prison, Paul was released on parole.

Throughout this whole ordeal, the most striking thing is how much the writer knew. Whoever it was had to have been well-connected, or able to access sensitive information somehow. Many of the accusations of crimes turned out to be true:

- Mary was indeed having an affair with the superintendent, though she claims that this started after the letters.
- The prosecutor in Paul's trial was named as the murderer of a pregnant woman. It transpired the prosecutor was having an affair with the woman, who died soon after, bearing *his* unborn baby.
- Dr Ray Carroll, who carried out the autopsy on Ron was accused of being a pedophile and was arrested in 1993 on 12 separate counts.
- Local embezzlement and corruption were repeatedly outed, much of which turned out to be true.

Either way, the writer hasn't been heard from since 1994, though is still technically considered a wanted individual. The possibilities of who it could be seems to be almost endless. Any of the citizens involved could have had some part to play; there could even be more than one writer.

The case of the Circleville Letters remains a captivating story with no ending confirmed, nor mastermind identified. Multiple documentaries have been created that examine the events and internet detectives continue to pore over all available evidence. After everything, however, the writer could well still be out there.

TWO LITTLE SHREKS!

For this next story, we're going to go far back in time to the 12th century, to a small village called Woolpit in Suffolk, England. As an extra bite of history, the name "United Kingdom" wasn't in effect at this point. In fact, it's a relatively recent name.

The joining of Scotland, Wales, England occurred in 1707, with Ireland joining in 1801, before leaving again. Northern Ireland joined in 1921. It is a little complicated, but at least now you know.

Woolpit is a tiny village in England that even today has a meagre population of about 2,000 people. The village gained its name from Old English, where it was called *wulf-pytt*, meaning "pit for trapping wolves."

The village is an old settlement, with one of the more remarkable churches that dates back almost 1,000 years and is a fascinating, intricate design.

Though it is very small, and though it is very old, Woolpit is home to one of the most remarkable sounding stories of the early Medieval period and one that remains something of a mystery today.

Sometime in the 12th century, likely around the reign of King Stephen (1135–1154), two children appeared in Woolpit to the villagers.

It was around harvest time and unnamed villagers discovered the children near the wolfpits that had given Woolpit its name. The children had never been seen before by any resident and they had no names that could be discerned.

The children were quite normal in appearance and seemed relatively healthy apart from one thing - they were green.

Yes, green.

And the children reportedly couldn't speak any recognizable language; it was instead some sort of nonsense that none of the villagers could identify.

They were wearing strange clothing that was also unrecognizable and distinctly not of Woolpit origin, nor anywhere in England as far as the people could work out. Both children were taken to the home of Richard de Calne, a local knight who had a manor some six miles north of the small village.

De Calne's experiences with the children inform most of our knowledge, as the source material written about this odd event was taken from his testimonies.

At the manor home, the children were offered sleeping quarters, drink, and food. The pair completely refused all food for several days, with a variety of vegetables, meats, and bread offered to them. It wasn't until some raw broad beans (fava beans) were offered that the pair broke their fast and consumed the broad beans with relish.

It was difficult in the earliest days of their discovery to communicate with them, they simply spoke a different language. Like asking a boomer to talk to a millennial, there's a barrier in the way and it can't be broken without extensive arguments.

As time went on, the children very gradually took to other food and moved away from their solitary consumption of broad beans. With adaptation to a more normal style of life and diet, the children also became less green, looking more like humans and less like Shrek's least favorite children by the day.

Unfortunately, the young boy (unnamed) was quite unwell and fell sick. In the 12th century, knowledge of how to cure illnesses was either nonexistent or just plain wrong. Whatever remedies or treatments were offered to the boy weren't effective, and he died. His sister, on the other hand, was baptized.

De Calne provided the remaining child with an education that far outstripped what most children were offered, and the girl quickly picked up the English language.

This was crucial for the investigation into who they were because she could now communicate where she'd come from. Unfortunately, her answer was somehow even less helpful than saying nothing at all.

The girl gave the following details, none of which have led to a conclusive answer:

- She called their home St. Martin's Land.
- The sun never shone in their homeland; light was more like twilight.
- Everything there was green.
- They had been herding cattle for their father when they were drawn by the sound of bells and found themselves by the wolf pit in Woolpit.

The green girl managed to integrate quite successfully into English life after this point and worked in de Calne's household as a servant. She didn't quite suit that life though and later married, under the name Agnes, to an official called Richard Barre.

So, shall we try to consider some answers as to what on Earth was going on here?

Unfortunately, contemporary scholars offer no explanation - if there was an investigation by local officials or anybody else, no answer was found.

More modern historians (amateur and professional) have weighed in, however. Some have argued that the story isn't worth investigating because no answer will be found, and we have no way of verifying what those in the 12th-century wrote about the event.

Others have argued that the children are aliens and aliens are now living among us. Many more historians think that the whole tale is a "garbled account" of a real event, meaning the children may have been kidnapped or drugged and their account was misunderstood by the adults.

The story has also had an impact on medieval folklore, and the green children are linked with the *Babes in the Wood*, a popular English children's tale.

The most credible and possible story is that the children were the children of Flemish immigrants who had been killed. Flemish people came from modern-day Belgium and spoke a language that's very different from English.

Flemish migrants arrived in England in the early 12th century and were persecuted soon after, which accelerated with the ascension of King Henry II in 1154. Due to these attacks on the Flemish, the children may have been part of an isolated, small community that wandered near Woolpit.

From there, the children could have become lost, or their community may have been wiped out, and they stumbled into Woolpit. Weary and Flemish, they'd have looked and sounded different to the English and could easily have confused the good people of Woolpit.

Of course, as ever when considering early Medieval history, it's difficult to completely trust what we've been told, and there are holes everywhere in the timeline of this incident. Not enough people were able to write and record their stories, so a lot has been lost in time.

I guess all we can say is, if you happen to see some little green people, don't panic and out them as aliens - they may just be Belgian.

DID ANYONE BRING A MAP?

Hiking and mountaineering are dangerous pastimes, or at least they can be. In the 2020s, Mount Everest has become a remarkably popular attraction for rich Westerners who fancy themselves as expert climbers and want to scale the most infamous mountain on the planet, take a wonderful selfie, and come back as some sort of fitness guru in their far more habitable environments at home.

Everest is now so popular that there are, at times, queues to climb up the mountain. Most don't make it too far and are discouraged and turn around, as it is quite difficult, but the queues make the whole situation even more dangerous. Each year people die on the mountain, and the number is increasing.

If you're thinking about becoming one of the great modern explorers, or possibly you're thinking about mountaineering because "everyone goes to France," read the following story about the outcome of a 1959 exploration of the Ural Mountains in Russia.

The story opens with a group of Russian hikers, who began a trip on January 27, 1959. The group initially consisted of eight men and two women, but one had to turn back early into the trip due to health concerns.

All the hikers were well-educated people, with most being university students studying at the Ural Polytechnic Institute, doing clever degrees like Radio Engineering (unlike History degrees, which only get you as far as writing this book).

As well as being super smart, they were all Grade-II hikers, with ski tour experience. This expedition was not their first rodeo, and the party had plans to go for their Grade-III upon their return. This journey to the mountains was essentially a bit of practice.

The group's leader was Igor Dyatlov, and it was dubbed the Dyatlov Party.

Igor Dyatlov had told his sports club that the party would send a telegram once they'd finished their hike on February 12. He warned them that there was a chance that it could be a day or two later, but by February 15 the families of the party still had heard nothing and grew concerned.

By February 20, a rescue party was ordered, with support from the army and police forces as well as experienced volunteers. They were worried that something had gone dreadfully wrong. How could the group not have finished yet?

They had every right to be concerned.

On February 26, the rescue party located the Dyatlov party's tent, which had been abandoned and severely damaged. The rescue party was puzzled by the state of the campsite. The tent was half torn down and covered in snow. Furthermore, all the group's belongings and shoes had been left behind. Later investigations concluded the tent fabric had been cut from the inside.

Leading from the campsite, nine sets of footprints could be identified in the snow, all showing people either wearing socks or nothing on their feet at all - the footprints led into a nearby wood, almost a mile away.

The investigators sprang into action, desperate to find survivors, if there were any. They came to the next sign of the Dyatlov party underneath a huge Siberian pine tree: clear remnants of a fire. Two bodies were found nearby and were immediately identified as members of the party.

They were dressed only in their underwear, with no shoes on. Between the abandoned camp and the pine tree, three further bodies were discovered in positions that clearly indicated they were attempting to return to the camp but didn't make it.

The remaining party members were found - after a further two months of investigation - under 13 feet of snow, 82 yards away from the pine tree where the first bodies had been located.

It's a grizzly tale, but not necessarily that mysterious in the first instance.

Hiking in dangerous environments leads to catastrophe all the time. Many of the hikers had clearly died from hypothermia; the temperatures would have been far below freezing and they had clearly been taken by surprise to have found themselves outside and far from their camp, inadequately prepared. But there lies the first mystery.

Why had they gone outside in such a rush?

The second mystery came after a series of medical examinations. All hikers were presumed, at first, to have died from exposure to the cold environment. However, that narrative began to shift. By May 1959, it was found that three of the hikers had suffered fatal injuries, meaning something had happened to physically harm them enough so it killed them.

One hiker had serious skull damage, while two others had been dealt major chest fractures. The inquests found that these injuries were the cause of death, not hypothermia. Strangely, none of these serious injuries and fractures had an outside wound, almost like they had been crushed, leading to massive internal damage.

So, here's the second question: How did three of the hikers incur such major injuries?

"What the hell happened then? You ask. So, let's get into it.

A Yeti

Let's get this one out of the way. Some journalists and more interesting individuals were convinced that the deaths were caused by the actions of, and were proof of, a Yeti. This is a large humanoid creature, covered with white hair, which can tear human beings' limb from limb.

Yetis are a hidden mystery in themselves, with some cultures convinced of the existence of these ape-like abominations, even going so far as to believing they have magical powers. One of the hikers had lost her tongue somehow; perhaps the Yeti had eaten it after its successful attack on the party?

Even if you accept the existence of Yetis, this explanation doesn't quite line up. The humans had no external injuries beyond one hiker with a cut on his forehead. Surely a crazed creature of the lost world would have inflicted more external damage or even consumed a full human - if it was a cheat day.

Avalanche

The original theory that the authorities came to after their investigation is a sensible one and there's plenty of evidence to back it up.

All mountaineers and hikers in remote regions fear avalanches. Avalanches can bury you and your equipment many feet under the ground within seconds, rendering you helpless and facing an inevitable, slow death.

Perhaps the group had cut their way out of the tent, as snow began to fall on it, launching into an emergency evacuation. They'd been sleeping, so in their panic, didn't manage to properly clothe themselves, and ran to the safety of the trees.

From here, they made a fire but were too cold and froze to death in the night. The group of four with miscellaneous injuries were caught in a subsequent avalanche and buried.

The missing tongue could have been eaten by anything, such as some small scavenging animal.

It sounds plausible and makes the actions of the party less irrational. They seem to have taken a lot of recommended actions that can help survival in avalanches. However, there are a few problems with the avalanche theory:

- There were no obvious signs of an avalanche near their campsite. If the last group was indeed buried by an avalanche, they would have suffered far greater injuries than they had and would likely have been swept away.
- More than 100 expeditions had been conducted to the region since the incident and none ever reported any conditions that might cause an avalanche.
- If a very specific avalanche had occurred, its path would have gone past the tent. The tent, however, had collapsed from the side, not the possible avalanche path.
- The party's experience in skiing and hiking would have stopped them from choosing to camp anywhere near a known avalanche risk.

Katabatic wind

A rare phenomenon that can be fatal, Katabatic Wind is a wind that carries high-density air down a slope. The wind is very fast and has been known to kill people before. Such a violent wind could have forced the hikers out of their tent to seek refuge toward the tree line.

Military tests

The Soviet military had been testing parachute mines near the site around early 1959. It is possible that the military wasn't aware of the civilian presence and let off mines, which surprised the party into leaving their tent quickly.

They may have then become disorientated, while a few suffered impact injuries from the mines.

This theory alleges a series of cover-ups from the military and possible radioactive weaponry in use. However, the papers relating to the Dyatlov incident have all been declassified and released and show no signs of military involvement.

An avalanche remains the most plausible theory but is also so easily disproved. The incident is still under investigation and is constantly analyzed by internet would-be detectives (not detectives), detectives (real detectives), and Russian officials. All you can take from this mystery is that it's dangerous to go outside, so stay indoors and order a pizza.

USELESS OR IMPORTANT?

What about a mystery that doesn't explicitly involve death or crime? You've got it!

If you are or were a parent of a young child, then you will only be too aware of the constant stream of nonsense artistic projects that your little sprogs will happily bring you on a regular basis.

With great pride, they'll present a painting they've done at elementary school of a little potato creature with stalks for legs, or they might delight in raving to you about their imaginary friend and the mysterious lands that exist beyond the closet.

It's always wonderful and hilarious, but let's be honest, they're talking a lot of rubbish and if they weren't your child, you'd put that painting in the garbage so quickly that they'd still be telling you which potato is you.

But nonsense artistic projects have always been made by those with a more inventive mind than most. Entire worlds have been conjured up by the writers of yester year and some, including J.R.R. Tolkien, even invented several languages, such were the depths of their fantastical intellect.

There was some such thought-provoking intellectual dwelling in 15th-century Europe, who toiled away at a piece of "work" that has led historians down a dark corridor of intellectual mystery.

Each door of this corridor leads to more questions than answers, and you leave it knowing far less than when you walked in. It's the same exercise as binge-watching two seasons of *Keeping Up with the Kardashians*. The piece of "work" we're referring to is the Voynich Manuscript.

Put simply, the Voynich Manuscript is either a piece of old twaddle, or it might be one of the most important works ever put to paper. The problem is, we simply don't know either way.

The manuscript was constructed sometime in the early 15th century. Carbon-dating the manuscript has given a date range of 1404–1438.

Historians are kind of sure that the writer was from Italy, but we're using the phrase "kind of" here to mean "they're about three out of ten sure."

The whole thing is approximately 240 pages long, but it's thought that some are missing, meaning it's currently both useless and incomplete. Text is written from left to right, so it's likely European, and most pages are adorned with fantastical drawings, diagrams, symbols, and pictures.

The Voynich Manuscript isn't written in any known language; it's written in a script now called *Voynichese* to give it a name, and no one knows what it says.

Many of the drawings are of non-existent things. Approximately half of the manuscript appears to be made up of the discussion of things herbal, and there are a great many herbal illustrations.

The illustrations are drawn in different ways, some of which are not typical of Medieval Europe, which makes identifying what has been drawn quite difficult. Some great excitement came from the identification of a sunflower and a pepper plant in the 1940s, which led some to believe that the manuscript writer may have been involved in some travel to America.

However, this isn't generally accepted, and many disagree that the illustrations are even of sunflowers or pepper plants. It's mostly now thought that if there are any real-life herbs in the manuscript, they're few and far between, with seemingly 99% of them being made up, accompanied by long paragraphs of *Voynichese*, which presumably detail them.

The writer or curator has also spent a great deal of time drawing out astrological and cosmological diagrams. They show star patterns and galaxies, some of which are found in other Renaissance or Medieval writings, or at least look very similar. However, for all the minor identifications of real groups of stars, much of it is indecipherable and seems to be of made-up star systems of astrological events.

Zodiac signs are also shown in the manuscript and seem to be the normal zodiac signs (Gemini, Leo, Cancer, etc.) depicted in unusual ways or orders. Humans and animals are also shown in the manuscript.

Some animals are mythical creatures such as dragons or are completely unidentifiable as anything seen elsewhere in Medieval drawing. The people are also referred to as "nymphs" by many art historians and look human but maybe aren't supposed to be.

At this point, I'm hoping that you're a little bit confused about this manuscript and are struggling to work out anything about it. If you are, that's good, because it is confusing.

The whole manuscript is baffling and there are so few answers as to what any of it might mean. Naturally, it's the subject of ongoing investigation and interest from historians. It would help if we knew anything about where it came from, but our history of its ownership starts almost 200 years after its creation, with an alchemist from Prague called Georg Baresch.

Baresch was interested in the manuscript and sought out its meaning from scholars in 17th-century Prague but to no avail. The work was shifted around Europe for a while until 1912 when Wilfrid Voynich purchased it at a discreet auction of religious and interesting historical artifacts by the Society of Jesus.

Voynich was a Polish collector and businessman. He owned one of the world's most successful rare book businesses and saw the manuscript as something of interest. He became obsessed with the manuscript and spent seven long years attempting to bring it to the attention of scholars and went to great lengths to discover more about its origins himself. Voynich died in 1930 having gained no useful information about it, though his name became attached to it.

The manuscript was inherited by his wife, who left it to her friend, who sold it to a book dealer. Finding no one to sell it to, the book dealer donated it to Yale University in 1969, which has held it to this day.

Obviously, we know nothing about the manuscript's contents due to its indecipherable script. Scholars have innumerable theories about what the text could be, with the more likely ones being:

a) The text is written in cipher - a systemized code known to the author, obscuring some meaningful and important text in the mysterious Voynich alphabet.
b) It's Latin but written in some shorthand, abbreviated way that wasn't acceptable to the scholars of the time, so the work would have been dismissed.

c) The manuscript is mainly useless, but within it holds the scientific understanding of the time. The writer might have concealed experiments or work in the text, such as every third word being relevant and the word to read.

d) The script is a natural language, which is a language that occurs naturally in a human community through use, repetition, and change. Somewhere along the line, the language has been lost, leading it to be completely unreadable.

All of these are real hypotheses that are yet to be disproven or proven by any credible theory.

The Voynich manuscript remains undeciphered and a source of genuine frustration for many scholars. Underpinning all the work, the thousands of hours that have gone into the manuscript, the many owners over its life, the carbon dating, the academic papers, and the art historian's analysis is the very real chance that it is a hoax.

It would be horrible, but the more that the manuscript eludes understanding, the more that the word "hoax" rears its ugly head.

The whole thing, all 240 pages might be a complete waste of time. Someone in 14th-century Italy may very well have simply sat down and, for fun, written out some useless document containing their wonderful little doodles and a nonsense alphabet.

There may be no useful information, or any information at all. In 2007, an Austrian researcher, Andreas Schinner, comprehensively concluded the work was gibberish as the placement and repetition of words pointed, statistically, to its meaning as nothing.

However, in 2021, Yale University published evidence that there are consistent patterns of repeating words that show conclusively the document contains text with meaning and isn't drivel.

Let's just stop here. This piece of work, encompassing artistic talent and a great deal of dedication, has plagued the interest of scholars throughout the ages.

Computers have analyzed the document, mathematicians and lexicographers have examined the words, and historians have traced its ownership back as far as can be traced. Yet we are *still* no closer to having any idea of what the darn thing is about!

It's a great mystery. One for the ages, and long may it continue. The day that the manuscript is understood will be a sad day for curiosity and will also render this chapter useless.

HOLD THE LEAD TIGHTLY!

What would you say the saddest, most unhappy animal in the world might be? Realistically, the answer is the human being. We're both blessed with an almighty intellect as well as cursed with the knowledge of death and the limitless expanse of time.

This combination can make human beings quite sad…, and then we decided to live in a way that necessitates some people doing well and others less well. So, we probably take the crown for the saddest animal – Boo Hoo, go us!

However, from there you might struggle. The donkey comes to mind because of the cartoon *Winnie the Pooh*, where Eeyore (the donkey) possesses a rather morose outlook on life, despite the relentless optimism of Pooh bear.

You may well have looked at the seemingly constantly downturned, sad eyebrows of a racoon or watched a video of one washing cotton candy in water, and seeing it melt in front of them. If you haven't, stop reading and YouTube it now! It'll break your little heart and it's hilarious.

Polar bears also have a sad air about them. Every day seems to be a fight for survival for the polar bear, with their environment dying away and food scarcity only getting worse.

Yet what if the answer, all along, was dogs?

I know precisely what you're thinking: "Surely not! Dogs have endless joy within them. Every day is a party for a dog, and they certainly aren't the saddest animals!" Well, you might be correct, but if you take your beloved poochie to Dumbarton in Scotland, make sure you're holding onto the lead tightly.

Dumbarton is a town on the river Clyde, a river written about in romantic Scottish poetry and sung about in traditional folk songs that stretches back well past the 19th century.

Dumbarton has a population of about 20,000 and its existence as a settlement, dates at least as far back as the Iron Age (1200 BCE), which makes it at least 11 times as old as the United States of America. We are concerned with one aspect of its history, which is the acquisition of the Overtoun Farm by a wealthy industrialist called James White in 1859.

White had big plans for the farm and set about major construction works to improve his new residence. He constructed Overtoun House, which you can go and see should you ever find yourself in the beautiful town of Dumbarton.

The house was a sprawling manor, intended as a country retreat for White and his family, which was left to his son upon his death in 1884.

His son John (very inventive names, fellas, well done) moved into the estate in 1891 and began expanding it, which included constructing the Overtoun Bridge, which would provide a way to cross a waterfall.

The bridge was gorgeous and the walk from the manor was now more pleasant and scenic. Although beautiful, the Overtoun Bridge is not known by the locals for its lovely walks or gorgeous views, however. It's not even known as the Overtoun Bridge! It has a far more sinister name…

The dog suicide bridge

Since at least the 1950s, the Overtoun Bridge has been the site of an inordinate number of doggy deaths. Some locals will insist that hundreds of dogs have thrown themselves with great vim from the bridge, plummeting to their deaths in the ravine that sits 49 feet below. Others state the toll isn't in the hundreds at all, but it is completely undeniable that many dogs have jumped off the bridge or have slipped off.

Most dogs (and indeed humans, but we'll get to that) that fall from Overtoun Bridge die upon impact with the hard ground or rocks that lie underneath. Those dogs that do survive face a hindered, shortened life.

There is even one recorded instance of a dog leaping from the bridge, smacking into the rocks, running up the slope - and then jumping off the bridge again!

As well as the doggy death, the bridge has also been the location of some grizzly human tragedy.

The bridge witnessed several suicides over the last 130 years and in 1994, a paranoid schizophrenic called Kevin Moy completed infanticide (the killing of his baby son) after he was convinced that the child was the reincarnation of the devil. Moy was subsequently placed in a mental health hospital where he remains for his safety and that of others.

Overtoun Farm is supposedly a site of druid cult practice. The Druids were religious leaders who, at a time, prevalently practiced a sort of dark religion in the countries that now make up the United Kingdom.

They're often associated with a sort of black magic particularly carried out in Scotland, Wales and West England.

Druidic involvement or not, we need some answers as to why the bridge is home to so many bizarre leaps of faith from man's best friend. As always, there are several theories and none have been fully proven yet, but one of them surely must be right and can reveal why these dogs are leaping like lemmings.

1. Supernatural causes

You simply can't have a place of death without someone claiming that there's supernatural involvement, and why not? Around 41% of Americans believe in ghosts, with 20% being unsure and 43% believing in demons. You might say "Yes, but that's Americans, we're talking about" and to that I say, Americans are the ones who are polled about this sort of thing; the Scottish are asked far more important questions. The point is, many people believe in the paranormal and think that there is more to this world than meets the eye, and there are stories in this vein about Overtoun Bridge.

Some locals have said that the wife of James White haunts the bridge, possessing unresolved fury at some injustice in her past. The story is substantiated by the behavior of many of the dogs and the precise location of much of the jumping. Fanatics have pointed out that dogs tend to jump from the exact location from which Kevin Moy threw his infant son, which some say is an indication that a spirit haunts that exact spot, or that some demonic entity takes hold of beings there. In 2014, Alice Trevorrow lost her Springer Spaniel Cassie at the bridge and was sure something was wrong with the area:

"Me and my son walked towards Cassie, who was staring at something above the bridge..., she definitely saw something that made her jump. There is something sinister going on, it was so out of character for her."

While it's difficult to prove supernatural forces, the bridge is undoubtedly spooky and has people wondering.

2. Smell

A compelling argument that has been investigated by several organizations and a documentary maker is that the dogs are strongly attracted by some intense smell, which causes them to launch into investigation and their untimely death. If you've walked a dog before, you will be aware of how quickly their mind can be turned by the waft of something delicious..., or even something that smells of poop.

Dr David Sands, who investigated the bridge suicides in the 2010s, was convinced of the presence of mink in the ravine. Mink had been brought to Scotland for farming in the first half of the 20th century, and mink farming was certainly active in the 1960s in the region.

Many minks were released into the Scottish countryside, either accidentally or deliberately, and now live in the undergrowth in plentiful numbers. Mink urine is a strong scent, and precisely the sort of smell of which a dog would love to sniff. If minks, otters, or rats are scurrying around underneath the bridge, some dogs may very well follow their nose to their doom.

The Royal Society for the Protection of Birds also carried out experiments on whether dogs would hurry toward the scent of mink when placed in proximity to mice and squirrels, with seven out of ten strongly favoring the mink.

It's worth pointing out, however, that no investigation has confirmed this theory of an overwhelming smell that takes hold of dogs. Many feel that if that were the case, more dogs would have jumped to their deaths. The dogs don't share a characteristic of being poorly trained. Some are well-behaved pups who would normally seek confirmation from their owner before doing anything, while others are more carefree.

3. The environment

The last theory, again explored by Dr David Sands, is that there's a combination of factors that lead dogs not to see the danger of jumping.

Sands says that the path can be disorientating for the dogs, which has gentle slopes at points. As the bridge is in the air, it also experiences the effects of strong crosswinds, which bring new smells to the bridge, as well as confusing dogs who are ahead of their owner.

Furthermore, the ravine is covered in dense foliage and trees, which obscures much of the drop. Dogs, with their limited capacity for understanding, probably can't see how far the drop is. Lastly, walkers are forever staring over the edge of the bridge and dogs look to human behavior for clues on how to behave themselves. If dozens of walkers are gawping over the edge, the dog might very well do the same and risk losing their footing.

Unfortunately, no amount of investigation has yet confirmed why the bridge is such a sight for dog suicide. Following Dr

David Sands's hypotheses, the Royal Society for the Protection of Birds' - investigations, and the Scottish Society for the Prevention of Cruelty to Animals - experiments, there's just no proven answer yet.

The only conclusive thing we can say is that the dogs probably aren't knowingly killing themselves. There are very few instances of animals ever trying to accelerate their demise. Animals are often aware of their incoming death, with elephants taking long walks in the days preceding their death to a sort of "graveyard" to die in a particular spot.

Owners often report pets going off their food and retiring to sleep early, to peacefully pass on. Something is causing the dogs to jump, and it's not an overwhelming feeling of misery; it's probably something that's luring them into the ravine.

ONE-WAY TICKET TO WEALTH AND PROSPERITY, PLEASE!

Some younger readers of this book perhaps don't remember the time before the horrific incident that was the airplane hijackings of September 11, 2001.

So revoltingly fresh is their youth that they may have been born a long time after the event and wonder why every old person bangs on about 9/11 so much. Well, aside from being a watershed moment for so many reasons on an international level, for the average flier, it also introduced far greater security at airports and slowed down the whole process of flying. And, naturally, we like to complain about that.

Now, especially in America, going through security to get on a plane is a stressful and a full-on affair. Security checks involve all sorts of scanners that attempt to identify illicit substances, bombs, weapons, or other illegal products, as well as necessitating the employment of literally thousands of officers who perform more…, personal inspections if required.

In the decades before 2001, flying was a bit more relaxed. It was taken seriously and there were security checks, but it was generally more chilled out.

Right up until the 1990s, customers (ideally children, not fully grown adult children) might have even had the chance to go to the cockpit and see the operation room of the plane and get to speak to the pilots.

That is literally illegal in the 21st century. Yes, you are no longer permitted to go into the room where they fly the thing that, if it crashes, will kill everyone on board.

Ultimately, it's probably because of this more *laissez-faire* attitude to aviation security that America witnessed one of the most remarkable aviation crimes ever. The disappearance of D. B. Cooper.

The story of D.B. Cooper is a mystery, yet we know almost everything about it. In this chapter, we'll bring you the story in a series of mini chapters that paint the timeline as we understand it, with all the detail that you need. In short, however, this is the story:

- A man bought a one-way ticket for a flight.
- When on board, he revealed a bomb and made demands of the crew.
- The crew relayed these demands to the authorities.
- The plane landed and refueled, where all the other passengers got off. The man was given what he demanded.
- The plane took off again, and while in the air, the man jumped out and was never seen again.

Part I

It was Thanksgiving Eve in 1971, that is, November 24.

Northwest Orient Airlines had a desk set up at Portland International Airport, and a man approached the desk carrying a black briefcase. The man bought himself a one-way ticket on a short 30-minute trip north to the Seattle-Tacoma International Airport, under the name of Dan Cooper. He was a White man, mid-40s with dark hair and brown eyes, and he was wearing a dark business suit with an equally dark raincoat. In other words, Dan Cooper didn't look hugely remarkable; just another businessman taking a trip home for Thanksgiving.

Cooper boarded the flight carrying his briefcase and a brown paper bag. He ordered himself a bourbon and 7-Up, I guess because he had a foul taste in beverages. The plane was carrying 37 passengers and had a crew of six, made up of three flight attendants and three operators of the plane. Everything was going well, the plane set off when it was supposed to set off and rocketed into the sky, destined to bring everyone on board to their Thanksgiving celebrations on time. That is, until shortly after take-off when Cooper turned to flight attendant Florence Schaffner and handed her a note.

Schaffner, as a flight attendant, was well used to lonely businessmen seeking extra-marital company, especially around the holidays. She popped the note into her purse without examining it, assuming it was a phone number and not wanting to hurt the gentleman's feelings. Cooper leaned over to Schaffner and said:

"Miss, you'd better look at that note. I have a bomb."

Schaffner's blood ran cold. She read the note, written with a felt-tip pen, which said both very little and everything at once:

I HAVE A BOMB IN MY BRIEFCASE AND WANT YOU TO SIT BY ME

Schaffner returned the note and sat next to Cooper. She then asked to see the bomb in his briefcase, wanting to ensure that this wasn't some elaborate and misjudged joke. Cooper opened the briefcase to reveal what looked like eight cylinders of dynamite attached to wires and a battery. The presumably terrified flight attendant did a fantastic job of remaining professional and calm. Rather than amplifying the ordeal by screaming or attempting to remove the bomb from Cooper's possession, she simply sat and listened to his demands, writing them out exactly on a piece of paper:

1. *$200,000 in a knapsack*
2. *Two front parachutes*
3. *Two back parachutes*
4. *The money must be in negotiable American currency.*

Cooper then directed Schaffner to the captain and asked her to relay his demands. She went to the captain and informed him of the developing events, and he requested that she stay in the cockpit with them to record everything as it was unfolding.

The captain was aware that there would be some questioning later, and it might be germane to have an accurate story to which to refer. Schaffner sat in the cockpit while flight attendant Tina Mucklow sat with Cooper to act as a liaison between him and the pointy end of the plane.

From here it all went rather calmly, with Cooper making a few more requests of Seattle:

> *Upon landing in Seattle, the fuel trucks will meet the plane and all passengers will remain seated, while the money is collected by Tina Mucklow. Once Cooper is in possession of the money, the passengers will be released, at which point the parachutes must be brought on board.*

And so, it continued. The FBI said that they would cooperate with his demands, and the president of Northwest Orient asked that the crew completely comply with Cooper.

Mucklow sat next to him as the plane circled overhead, waiting for the FBI to assemble $200,000, which was difficult as ATMs only let you take out $400 at a time.

(That's a joke, of course. Though ATMs were invented around 1971, they weren't in regular use. Also, the FBI had the money and wouldn't need to use an ATM!)

Cooper, according to Mucklow, seemed to recognize the landscape below them and remained exceptionally calm. He discussed local geography and the layout of Tacoma with her, and she said he was perfectly pleasant and never seemed rude or impatient.

He assured her that the choice of airline wasn't personal, it just suited him. Cooper quizzed Mucklow about where she was from (Minnesota) and offered her a cigarette - Mucklow had quit smoking but accepted anyway. A decision that no doctor could begrudge her.

The ransom had been gathered and photographed, while the parachutes were secured from a nearby skydiving school.

Cooper's insistence on two sets of parachutes was a stroke of genius; in doing so, he insinuated that someone would be coming with him, and so there would be no point in tampering with the equipment. The FBI wasn't to know that Dan Cooper was planning a solo trip.

Part II

At about quarter to six, the plane finally landed after the captain had been told that the money and parachutes were ready. While the plane refueled, the passengers remained seated, and Mucklow left the plane to collect the ransom money from Northwest Orient's operations manager. She brought the money back to him and he released the passengers, but the total crew remained on the plane.

Cooper counted the money as the passengers filed out. Presumably they weren't cheerily met with "Thank you for flying Northwest Orient, we hope you had a pleasant flight!"

Feeling the tension in the air, Mucklow jokingly asked if she could have some dosh, to which Cooper readily agreed. He handed her a huge wad of cash and told her she could have it - to which Mucklow responded in such a cool manner that she'd have made Ryan Gosling look like the Nutty Professor by comparison. Mucklow informed Cooper that it was against company policy to accept tips from customers!

Very cool, Mucklow, very cool indeed.

Mucklow went back out to collect the parachutes, as per Cooper's request, and brought them back on board. She gave the instructions that were printed to Cooper, but he discarded them, clearly familiar with how to operate the equipment. The remaining flight attendants Schaffner and Alice Hancock asked Cooper if they could leave the plane as well, to which he said, "Whatever you girls would like," so they left.

The refueling took longer than was expected, and Cooper used the time to talk with the crew and to deliver his flight plan, which involved a southeast course toward Mexico City at the slowest possible speed it could travel at without stalling. With the captain, he discussed where to refuel, and Cooper demanded the exit door remain open with its airstair deployed once airborne.

Part III

At 7:40 p.m., the plane took off once more, with Matlock remaining as the only flight attendant, the full operational crew still on board, and their solitary passenger, Dan Cooper. Once airborne, two fighter jets from a local Air Force base followed in such a pattern that they remained out of Cooper's vision.

Cooper requested Matlock's help in lowering the airstair, but she was frightened. Doing so was dangerous; she feared she might be sucked out of the plane and killed. Cooper eventually told her to go to the cockpit and close the curtains that separated Coach and First Class, to obscure her view of him. He told her not to return.

Matlock pleaded with Cooper to take the bomb with him, and he assured her that it would either be on his person, or it would be disarmed and left in the plane. Matlock went to the cockpit. Only four to five minutes had elapsed since take off. As she closed the curtain partition, she looked back at Dan Cooper, not knowing she'd be the last person to ever see him again.

At 8.00 p.m., a warning light flashed indicating that the airstair had been deployed.

The cabin asked Cooper through the intercom if he needed any assistance, and he merely replied "No." Thirteen minutes later, the aircraft's tail pitched upward dramatically, forcing a correction from the pilots to keep the flight level; this happened somewhere over Portland and is assumed that this was where Cooper left the plane.

Theories

So, that's the full story. The disappearance of D.B. Cooper is remarkable and unsolved. It's remained America's most famous aviation crime and Cooper is still technically wanted, though assumed dead by this point.

The FBI produced a profile of Cooper. With his knowledge of the area of Tacoma and Seattle, combined with his seemingly good knowledge of aircraft and parachutes, their profile concluded:

A military-trained parachutist and not a sports skydiver.

His age would have made him an outlier in any sports diving group and his disappearance/the sketches would have been noticed by any such group soon after. He exercised regularly and wasn't a heavy drinker, having only asked for one drink, which was spilled. Cooper likely smoked a pack of cigarettes a day, given how much he smoked on the flight (yes, it was a different time), and he was more intelligent than most criminals.

His name was not actually Dan Cooper, of course. That was an alias taken from a series of French-Belgian comic books that featured a hero pilot with the same name. As the books were never produced in England, the mystery man likely spent time in Europe, either on military duty or otherwise.

What happened to D.B. Cooper is unknown. Some FBI agents speculated at the time that he may not have survived the jump, and that if he survived, he would probably have suffered injuries upon landing. However, no money nor corpse was discovered despite extensive searches of the area, and it's believed he didn't have an accomplice to help him.

Other agents involved in the investigation think he survived and may have even slept in his own bed that night. It was very dark when he jumped, and no one saw him do so. He could have walked down the road holding his bag of money without being bothered by anybody en route.

After Cooper's hijacking, five copycat hijacks were carried out in the space of a few months, with all hijackers surviving their attempts (though being caught).

So, at the end of it all, the FBI drew up some suspects using their profile, but none were confirmed to be Cooper at all.

The agency can't even agree on whether he survived the jump or not. For all we know, Cooper could have made it across the border some days later and spent the rest of his life living on a beach in Argentina, with his newly acquired wealth and all the time he had left.

BUT WHAT ABOUT
THE POOR HORSE?

In 1920, America was at the beginning of what would be a prosperous decade following World War I. Europe would rely heavily on the USA to prop up their banks and help supply material goods to help the post-war recovery. "Money makes the world go round, the world go round', and America had all of the money. They were like your Dad in Monopoly: they owned most of the board, lots of the available money, and you're getting by with your light blue section that no one lands on.

All this money drove investment in America to new heights that wouldn't stop until the Wall Street Crash started on October 29, 1929. Wall Street in New York City was where the big bucks were made, and traders and tourists flooded the streets to be at the center of it all. The streets were alive with shouting, hand gestures, running businessmen, and carts - it was the perfect opportunity to make it big. It was also the perfect opportunity for someone to ruin it all.

The date was September 16, the lunchtime rush had just started, and the crowds were building. As the clock struck mid-day, a normal-looking man driving a normal-looking horse and cart passed along Wall Street. In front of the U.S. Assay Office (where precious metals are tested) and across the street from the headquarters of J.P. Morgan, one of the biggest investment banks ever, the cart came to a halt. It was the busiest part of the busiest place in America. The man descended from the cart and walked briskly into the crowd. No one took much immediate notice, why would you?

Within a minute, the cart - and unfortunately, the horse - exploded. There was total chaos. The blast had been caused by 100 pounds of dynamite and 500 pounds of heavy metal weights constructed from cast iron. Within seconds, bodies fell to the ground and the crowd turned, dazed, to witness the driver sprinting from the scene of the crime down a side street.

Thirty people (and one horse) were immediately killed by the explosion, while a further ten succumbed to their injuries in hospital soon after. Around 300 people were injured, with half being very serious or life-altering injuries. Beyond the human toll, $2 million worth of damage was caused to personal and public property, which is the modern-day equivalent of about $30 million. Trading ceased on Wall Street within 60 seconds and police officers descended on the scene to offer first aid and to hunt for the missing driver.

But it was all to no avail. The driver had vanished, and no one had managed to get a good look at him; plus, there were thousands of people at the scene. Many hundreds had already dispersed by the time that the police even knew they were looking for a suspect, so how were they supposed to quiz people who had already begun to head home?

The New York Stock Exchange was desperate to start trading the next day. Serious disruptions to financial activity weren't good, especially when there were very rich and powerful men who wanted to become even more rich and powerful. Overnight clean-up crews worked tirelessly, removing debris, bricks, dust, and presumably blood from the street so the Stock Exchange might open on time the following day, which it did. The problem, however, was that in doing so, all evidence left at the scene of the crime was cleaned away!

It took a short while for anyone at the Justice Department to even decide that this was an act of terrorism worth investigating.

Perhaps it was one of those strange incidents of spontaneously exploding horses? The cart had been parked in an area with no clear target, and most of the buildings of financial institutions were largely untouched. If this was some protest or attack on the Stock Exchange, it was a poorly executed one. Instead, innocent people - who weren't involved with the Stock Exchange at all - had been brutally killed for no apparent reason, so where to even start investigating?

The media jumped to action and began doing some investigations of their own. In this instance, investigating means "pointing at groups and accusing them." Every paper seemed to be accusing someone different. Due to the attack on these behemoths of capitalism, the communists were the first to be accused. Then the radical socialists and anarchists of America seemed the most likely. However, these groups weren't really known to use bombing as a weapon to make their point.

Luckily, the police were able to rule out an accidental bombing a day after the incident when flyers were found in a post office box that read:

"Remember, we will not tolerate any longer. Free the political prisoners, or it will be sure death for all of you."

The flyers were the best lead that any department had managed to secure. It was thought that they belonged to a group that called itself the "American Anarchist Fighters," who had attempted to carry out similar bombings in 1919. American Anarchists were linked to international anarchist groups, who were vehemently against the institutions of government and the financial districts. The group felt that all of this grouping was one and the same and that political prisoners taken by the government should be released.

The Bureau of Investigation (now the FBI) went to every printer and anarchist organization that it could to locate who had printed the flyers. No stone was left unturned on the East Coast of America, but there wasn't a printer who remembered printing the flyers, nor an anarchist who knew about them. Initial suspicions pointed to Italian anarchist Luigi Galleani and his followers, known for his capacity for militantism. But Galleani had long ago fled the country, and so had many of his followers.

As the days turned to months and the months turned to years, hot leads ran cold, and dead ends appeared everywhere the Bureau searched. The best and most likely supposition is that it was indeed a group of anarchists, but no one truly knows. There's much evidence to support an individual bomber acting on their own, as the bomb was constructed of readily available materials that any American would have been able to buy. It wouldn't be the first, nor the last time, that an act of terrorism had been carried out by a loner looking to make headlines.

For America, this was one of its earliest confirmed terrorist attacks and was a viciously brutal one. Innocent civilians being targeted caused great fear and the ongoing conspiracy theories peddled by media outlets showed little sign of slowing as time passed by. To this day, internet conspiracists will swear that the whole thing was a government plot to turn people away from Wall Street. Others will tell you that it was Germans, furious about the outcome of the war and America's involvement in their post-war reparations.

Either way, it's a fascinating case of such a blatant attack being so expertly and subtly carried out. Given it's been more than 100 years since the attack, the perpetrators have gotten away with it. Out of everyone asked about the bombing, the one person who needed to be asked was running away while everyone else was trying to work out what had just happened.

THE IMPOSSIBLE STAR

I would now like you to pronounce the word **Pryzybylski**. Do it out loud if the moment takes you and you're not somewhere embarrassing like on a bus.

It's a tough word. A name actually, a Polish one to be precise, and it is pronounced like "Pshi Bill Skee." The name belongs, as does this story, to Antoni Pryzybylski, a Polish-Australian astronomer who, in 1961, discovered something bizarre about a star and had his name written into the great history of astronomy (also known as "looking-at-the-sky-ology").

Mr Pryzybylski worked at the Mount Stromolo Observatory and was, by all accounts, having a normal day at work. While observing a star with a quite unremarkable name of "hd101065" (catchy, isn't it?), he noticed something slightly odd about it. Pryzybylski studied the chemical composition of the star, and his conclusions were bizarre and certainly non-typical. The further he studied, more strange results emerged, and eventually the star attracted interest from other world-renowned astronomers. The star would become known as Pryzybylski's Star, and the study of this odd phenomenon still baffles astronomers six decades later.

Before we get into exactly what makes Pryzybylski's Star so odd, let's take a moment to simply acknowledge what a star *is*. Put simply, a star is a very large ball of bright, hot, and glowing matter (stuff) in space. Our Sun is our closest star, and hopefully you're aware that it is entirely necessary for our ongoing survival as a species. Stars tell us a great deal about the history of the universe and go through long life cycles, from their inception when gravity brings together many forms of gas, to their eventual collapse. Sometimes, when we're observing stars in the night sky, we're seeing something that is no longer in existence; they're just so far away that it takes millions of years for the light to travel to Earth.

Most stars are quite similar and are made up of the same sort of stuff, containing similar gases and chemical makeups. Some vary slightly, and some are like hd101065, or Pryzybylski's Star.

The first thing to mention is that Pryzybylski's Star is abundant in metals and elements that we have a very small amount on Earth. If you look at the periodic table…well, go on then! So, look at the periodic table, and you'll notice two lines of elements at the bottom of your screen that are positioned away from the larger groups of elements. The top line of those isolated two are called Lanthanides, otherwise known as the rare-earth metals, because they're so exceptionally rare.

You may ask "So what?", to this question. The reason that Pryzybylski was so taken by this particular star is because most stars are made up of hydrogen and helium, and usually comprise 98% of a star, with only 2% being other stuff. Much of the gas in a star is essentially the fuel that gives off the colossal amounts of heat that allow life to occur, such as it has on Planet Earth.

Pryzybylski's Star has an abundance of Lanthanides, and there's no acceptable reason why that is the case. No law of physics that we humans have come up with can explain the abundance of rare-earth metals, providing a head-scratcher for the last 60 years. The high concentration of Holmium is one of the biggest puzzles by far. The heavy metal is similar in density to Gold or Platinum but isn't well understood as there's not much of it on Earth and it's yet to be fully studied. Holmium hasn't been found on any other space body that has been analyzed or visited, except for Pryzybylski's Star. In fact, it seems that this particular star may well hold almost all of the Galaxy's Holmium.

However, this is merely a drop in the ocean. Pryzybylski's Star is home to many short-lived radioactive metals, which have a short half-life. A half-life is the time required for the radioactivity to be reduced by half of its initial value. If an element has a half-life of 30 years, then that means:

1. In 30 years, the amount of radioactive material is reduced to 50% of the original 100%.
2. Another 30 years, and it's now at 25%.
3. Another 30 years, and it now sits at 12.5%.
4. And so on, and so on until there is essentially no radioactivity at all.

When it comes to Pryzybylski's Star, we're concerned with Prometheum, which has a half-life of just over 17 and a half years. The Star has a *lot* of Prometheum, which is odd because after 177 years, Prometheum has pretty much completely decayed, as it's so short-lived. The Star hasn't lost any Prometheum, and simply seems to have a lot of it, even though it should be losing large amounts of it. The Star is an estimated 1.5 billion years old so the chances of us having caught sight of it in the 177-year long period where the Prometheum is all decaying is very, very slim. In fact, it's almost impossibly slim - it's slimmer than your knowledge of Prometheum probably was before reading this book.

So, there we have it: Pryzybylski's Star contains an overabundance of very rare metals that are too heavy to be formed by most stars. It also contains vast quantities of Prometheum, which should burn up in the blink of an eye, when considering the Star's life span. Something is probably replenishing the Prometheum supplies, but what? And exactly why is there so much rare metal there?

There are a few theories, which I'll try my absolute best to keep simple:

a) We don't know something yet. The Star is simply a very special type of star that we cannot yet understand and that's just how it is for now.

b) The star has a "pulsar companion," which provides extra radiation for the Star and helps it to create rare metals in its upper atmosphere. However, no pulsar companion has been discovered.

c) The star contains some very long-lived nuclear particles, which produce Prometheum.

d) An alien species is dusting the Star with Prometheum for some purpose that at this time, isn't clear to us.

It's all very complicated and the theory is far more complex than I want to go into in this book (also, after a point, I simply don't understand it). But the fact remains that Pryzybylski's Star is a bizarre anomaly that simply doesn't make sense and has eluded our greatest astronomers and physicists. It may be some time before we get an actual answer as to what's going on there, or we very well may never discover what's going on.

THE TRUE IDENTITY
OF JACK THE RIPPER

If you've ever visited London - in England (not London, South Africa or London, Venezuela or London, Tennessee or London, Arkansas or London, Nigeria or London, Canada or London, Belize or London, Myanmar or London, Pennsylvania or London, Missouri or London, West Virginia) - then you may very well have heard the phrase "Ripper Walks" thrown about. "Ripper Walks" are a particular type of attraction that can be found in Whitechapel, an area of London, which involves a historian (or at least a history buff) walking patrons around and telling them about the grizzly and mysterious events of 1888.

Notably, 1888 was the year in which the notorious killer known as "Jack the Ripper" brought terror to East London while simultaneously providing the very best true crime drama that every podcaster wishes they'd got to first. "Jack the Ripper" is merely a name given to an anonymous killer. No one knows for sure who the real killer was, but the name lives on in infamy, poisoning the image of Victorian London forever. When we think of that era, in every smog-filled street, lurking around the corner from the workhouse, we picture a tall, anonymous man, dressed in a dark suit and long coat, with a top hat completing the ensemble.

This is the story of what we know about Jack the Ripper and some theories as to his identity. Given that it's a story about a mass murderer, expect some violent imagery, though I'll do my best to avoid being too gruesome. If you're below the age of 18, be careful if googling further; the photographs may very well bring your breakfast back up.

For your interest, Britain in the 19th century was a country experiencing a colossal amount of change. It was the greatest superpower in the world, built on the backs of immoral colonization and centuries of naval dominance. With the Industrial Revolution in full swing, the people of Britain saw an influx of consumer goods and greater wages than they had ever seen before, with millions moving to cities where industry was the chief employer. Alongside this, Britain experienced massive amounts of immigration from Ireland and Eastern Europe, alongside many Jewish migrants escaping persecution in mainland Europe.

Migration and industry created wealth, but they also created poverty, with London experiencing great polarity between the poor and the rich. Infant mortality was hideously high, with 55% of children born in East London dying before the age of five. Multiple families sharing small living spaces had become commonplace. With extreme poverty came crime, with sex work, gambling, violence, alcoholism, and robberies becoming part of East London life, driving away businesses and prosperity. In short, the country was confused, frustrated, and divided by extreme inequality. The East End was seen as a den of iniquity and by the late 1880s, tensions were running high, with some calling for the inhabitants to be prosecuted for immoral crimes and moved out of London.

It's worth mentioning that the police force was new in England. Systems of managing crime had always been vague in the country, and the now-famous Metropolitan Police Service was in its infancy, possessing limited knowledge and tactics. And if you were going to commit a crime anywhere, you'd do it in the East End, because honestly, who'd notice?

Because of the vast amount of violent crime, there's some debate over exactly how many women were targeted by "Jack," with some estimates going as high as 11. However, it's generally accepted that there were five confirmed victims of the Ripper, all attacked in similar fashions and all suspected sex workers. These five became known to historians as the "canonical five," with detailed accounts and interviews carried out by the police providing a good picture of what seems to have happened to them.

Victim I

The first victim was discovered at 3:40 a.m. on August 31, 1888, and her name was Mary Ann Nichols. Nichols had had a difficult '80s, separating from her husband who resented paying her a weekly allowance, as was the requirement at the time. She'd lived with her father, worked in workhouses, and earned money through sex work. As her dependency on alcohol worsened, she struggled with homelessness in 1888 and, on the evening of August 30, set out to earn some money so that she could pay for her bed at a lodging house. Nichols was last seen heading toward Whitechapel Road, looking for patrons.

She was discovered by a "carman," or delivery driver, called Charles Cross who initially thought he was looking at a tarpaulin (a sort of heavy-duty canvas), but soon realized that it was a body. Nichols had been savaged, with several deep cuts to her neck, stomach, and genitals. Even with the rough reputation that the East End of London had, the sight was a stomach-turner and caused a ripple in the area around Whitechapel. Newspapers were quick to point to recent murders and the police were keen for any information that might lead to the eventual identification of the killer.

Victim II

It was a little over a week later, on September 8, that the next confirmed victim of The Ripper was found at approximately 6 a.m. by an elderly resident of 29 Hanbury Street. Her name was Annie Chapman. Annie also had experienced a traumatic time of things, in much the same way as Mary Ann Nichols. One of Annie and her husband's children was disabled, and they'd both taken strongly to alcohol to cope with the pressures of raising the child in difficult circumstances. They'd separated and Annie had found herself living in common lodging houses by 1888, an alcoholic, and surviving by selling crochet and flowers plus engaging in casual sex work.

Chapman was ill by early September, an illness that physicians believe would have killed her later that year. She was in complete disarray, struggling with addiction, poverty, and trauma. At the inquest into Chapman's murder, one Elizabeth Long testified under oath that she saw Chapman talking to a man at approximately 5:30 a.m. in the backyard of 29 Hanbury Street. She said the man was about 40 years old with dark hair, a shabby appearance, wearing a long coat, and maybe a felt hat. If this was true, she was the last person to see Chapman alive, and maybe one of the only people that saw the murderer.

Chapman had been murdered in a similar fashion to Nichols, with the same cuts to the throat. She'd also had organs removed from her abdomen, and the police noted the almost surgical precision by which she'd been eviscerated. The media were taken by the murder and obsessed with the mystery. Weeks passed after Chapman's murder and papers ran stories alleging that the murderer must have been caught and that this villain's tyranny was over.

'Dear Boss'

Then, on September 27, the Central News Agency of London received a letter written in red ink, allegedly from the murderer. It started "Dear Boss…" The letter made oblique references to "ripping" and mocked the police for their dogged but ultimately ineffectual attempts to catch the murderer. Referencing "whores," the letter gave some sort of identifier as to who the killer might be, or at least some inference about his character. He hated sex workers, and they were his intended victims, which matched the pattern of both Chapman and Nichols. The letter went on to say that he would kill soon and post the ears of the victim to the Metropolitan Police Service, before signing off "Yours Truly, Jack the Ripper." A new moniker had been given to the killer, and the media used it enthusiastically. It would only be three days until they had another incident to talk about.

Victims III and IV

Known as "the double event," September 30 saw two murders that have been attributed to the Ripper - the murders of both Elizabeth Stride and Catherine Eddowes.

Both Stride and Eddowes were sex workers. Unlike the other victims, however, Stride had been a long-term sex worker; the others had turned to sex work following various breakdowns in relationships.

On September 19, Stride was the first to be found at approximately 1.00 a.m. by Louis Diemschutz, a steward of the International Working Men's Educational Club. Diemschutz was driving his horse and cart, illuminated by lamplight, and saw a bundle on the ground which the horse veered away from sharply. Upon discovering a body, he quickly checked on his wife (ensuring she was alive), before investigating further. Stride was still bleeding from a huge wound across her neck, which suggests she had been killed mere moments before Diemschutz discovered her. Most Ripper experts now conclude that this was a hurried murder from the killer, and he felt the need to leave quickly to evade detection.

Forty-five minutes later, at 1:44 a.m., Eddowes was discovered in Mitre Square by Police Constable Edward Watkins, who was walking his "beat," which included the square. He had previously walked through the square at about 1:30 a.m. and was convinced that no such body was to be found then, which suggests that the Ripper had barely evaded discovery for the second time that night.

Eddowes had been brutally attacked, with severe damage done to her eyes and uterus, and with organs having been removed from her abdomen. A cigarette salesman by the name of Lawende was interviewed. He said he saw a man and a woman enter the square shortly after 1:30 a.m. but couldn't be certain that the woman was Eddowes, nor what the man looked like.

Victim V

On November 9, the last canonical victim was discovered in a fashion yet unseen by the Ripper. Her name was Mary Jane Kelly, and she was found in her bedroom in Spitalfields at 10:45 a.m. Kelly, like many of the canonical five, had been previously married but the marriage had broken down. By the time of her death, she was renting a single room without much furniture and was working as a sex worker to make ends meet. She was engaged in a relationship with Joseph Barnett, who had lived with her in the room, but moved out in late October after quarreling about Kelly allowing girls to stay in the room on cold nights. Barnett visited her on the night of the 8th for the last time.

Because Kelly was residing in a home with several lodgers, her activities were very well documented that night. She wasn't drunk nor in any real state of distress. Fellow resident Mary Ann Cox recalled seeing Kelly go into her room with a "stout, ginger man" just before midnight, though she was also spotted later in the company of a taller gentleman in the street. Residents were convinced that they'd heard a cry of "Murder!" at around 4.00 a.m., but the cry was only heard once and wasn't uncommon to hear in the East End.

Kelly was discovered by her landlord's assistant, who was visiting her to receive her late rent payments. She had been savaged so completely that she was hardly recognizable as Mary Jane Kelly at all. There was scarcely one part of her that had been left unmutilated. For the first and only time, crime scene photographs were taken of the sight; illustrations had been completed for the other canonical five.

After Mary Ann Kelly, it's believed that the Ripper's spree ended.

But why? And who was it?

Regrettably, there are no answers. Mainly because the police force of London wasn't developed enough in their methods to be able to track the killer, nor look much deeper than the surface of what they saw. Detectives at the time had several ideas, and historians have published books that claim to reveal the identity of Jack the Ripper, but there's no confirmed identification. It's very much the Holy Grail of true crime drama: Discover who the Ripper was, and you may well become a very wealthy person.

There are several theories about who it might have been and why the murders stopped, each very possible but unprovable:

1. Given the exact nature of the murders, with surgical style cutting and such, the Ripper may have been a doctor or scientist. However, the murders really weren't *that* surgical and seemed frenzied. This theory probably emerged because people were generally distrustful of doctors and modern science at the end of the 19th century.

2. The Ripper was a woman, who despised sex workers for some reason. Perhaps her husband had employed the use of a sex worker and had angered her. The theory doesn't explain many questions, however, such as knowledge of how to remove organs (given that women weren't permitted to be surgeons at this time), or how the Ripper evaded detection.

3. The Ripper was a migrant. Given the high levels of immigration from America and Europe into London, there was great suspicion of such people from London citizens.

An American actor, Richard Mansfield, who had starred in *Dr. Jekyll and Mr. Hyde* was a named suspect, in fact. However, this is probably because his character committed murders in the play. This theory also leaves questions regarding the Ripper's ability to evade the police. It's often thought that the killer must have had great knowledge of the East End of London and was thus likely born a Londoner.

4. It was Queen Victoria's grandson, "Eddy" the Duke of Clarence and Avondale. As suspicious as people were of poor migrants and a criminal underclass, they also distrusted the royal family. The theory goes that "Eddy" had run away to East London and had carried out the murders, which were then elaborately covered up by the establishment. However, there's little evidence to back this claim.

The list of theories and suspects is absolutely endless, and the identity of Jack the Ripper remains a mystery. Unfortunately, a lack of good policing and eyewitness accounts render all contemporary investigations almost useless. Given how much time has now passed, it's very unlikely that new evidence will be forthcoming in the case, and "Jack" will forever be an English horror tale. Also, so long as he's not discovered, the Ripper Walks can continue, so at least it keeps people in employment.

WANTED: ANY INFORMATION, AT ALL, PLEASE!

THE FIVE W'S OF SOLVING A CASE

WHO – no idea!

WHAT – murdered? Maybe?

WHY – no clue!

HOW – you've got me there!

WHERE – probably the beach! But maybe not.

Why is it that the word "mystery" is so synonymous with "murder"? Is it because they both start with an "M"? Probably not. Murder is just intrinsically interesting because it's something that most of us won't have anything to do with, thank God. When it happens, it's unusual, traumatic, and sometimes unresolved. While this book does its best to avoid banging on only about odd deaths, well…, here's another.

In Adelaide, Australia, there's a suburb called Somerton Park. It's mainly a residential area that comprises a beach, college, cemetery, and a now-defunct care home for children. There's not much to talk about regarding Somerton Park, but it has been home to a couple of tragic incidents and one huge mystery. The mystery seems to be trundling toward a resolution, though there are still many questions around the whole case that are yet to be resolved. The case is often known as "The Somerton Man," and starts on December 1, 1948, with the discovery of a body.

Local police were called at 6:30 a.m. to investigate a body found on the beach at Somerton Park. He was lying on his back on the sand, his head resting against the seawall, and his feet crossed over, legs extended. The man looked quite peaceful, and initially, it seemed obvious that he'd been sleeping or resting when he'd died. Eyewitnesses had seen the man on the beach the previous night, lying in the same spot - though no one investigated until the next morning. One couple claimed that they saw him reach his arm out at one stage, while another witness admitted that they were suspicious when the man failed to react to the many mosquitoes buzzing around his head.

The man had a few objects and detritus with him: an unlit cigarette, one unused rail ticket, a bus ticket from Adelaide, a comb, a half-empty (or half-full) pack of chewing gum, a cigarette pack that contained seven cigarettes not of the box brand, and a box of matches. There was nothing hugely interesting about the items, but an autopsy pointed to something more sinister:

> "There was congestion of the pharynx. The stomach was deeply congested...There was congestion in the second half of the duodenum. There was blood mixed with the food in the stomach. Both kidneys were congested, and the liver contained a great excess of blood in its vessels.... The spleen was strikingly large...about three times normal size...there was destruction of the center of the liver lobules revealed under the microscope."

No poison was discovered in the man's bloodstream, but the pathologist, Dr Dwyer, was certain that the man's death wasn't a natural one. Food consumed by the UDM (Unidentified Dead Man, I just made that up) wasn't suspected as poisonous, and irritatingly, no identification could be found on his person - which meant that no one knew how he died, how he got to Somerton Beach, and (for a long time, at least) who he was. The man was embalmed on December 10, with the police sure that there would be more to his story.

It took until January 19, 1949, for the next clue to emerge, and it was a big one. It somehow tells us a lot without telling us anything. Adelaide railway station staff discovered a suitcase that had been checked in on November 30, the day before the body was found on Somerton Beach. The suitcase was assumed to be the mysterious gentleman's and the police investigated. Inside the suitcase, they found:

- Size seven pair of red slippers

- A red dressing gown
- Pajamas
- Four pairs of underpants
- Shaving things
- A brown pair of trousers, with sand in the cuffs
- A screwdriver
- A pair of scissors, with sharpened points
- A square of zinc
- A stenciling brush
- A table knife cut to work as a short and sharp instrument
- Some type of thread from Barbour, not found in Australia.

All name tags had been removed from clothing. Name tags were very commonplace in the post-war era, and there had been evidence that tags had been deliberately cut away. There were a few labels that referred to the name "T. Keane," but there'd been no report of a Keane missing from any English-speaking country, and police decided that it was unlikely to be the man's name given how carefully the other labels had been removed. They figured "Keane" was either irrelevant or a deliberate diversion. The fact that there were no spare socks seemed relevant somehow to the police, but regardless, the whole affair remained odd and unrevealing.

An inquest followed, where several discoveries were revealed. Firstly, the man's shoes had been recently polished and buffed - hardly what one would expect from someone who'd been pacing around the beach all day. This helped to inform the theory that the body was moved to Somerton Beach, rather than him dying there, which also explained the lack of vomiting, which would have likely happened had he been poisoned. Despite this theory, however, there was no conclusive evidence that poison had been used, and some locals were sure that they'd seen the man moving on the beach.

During the inquest, in June 1949, a small piece of paper was discovered sewn into the man's trousers. This part of the tale makes it read like some detective drama from the 1970s and has baffled the police and enticed the interest of every true crime podcaster and oddball. The tiny piece of paper bore upon it, two words:

"Tamám Shud."

Officials at the public library were able to assist and positively confirmed that the words "Tamám Shud" meant "ended" or "finished" and were found on the last page of *Rubaiyat of Omar Khayyam*. The book is a translation of several poems from Omar Khayyam, an 11th-century Persian poet and astronomer.

After a public appeal, a gentleman brought a copy of the book to the police; the book had a small section cut out of it on the last page, where the words "Tamám Shud" should have been. The man who brought it in has never been officially identified; the police instead gave him the pseudonym of "Ronald Francis," and we don't know who he was. In fact, we don't really know why the book emerged at all. Most reports agree that it was found in an unlocked, parked car near the beach where the body had been found.

Further still, the book contained five lines of text scribbled onto the back page, which read as such:

WRGOABABD
~~*MLIAOI*~~
WTBIMPANETP
✗
MLIABOAIAQC
ITTMTSAMSTGAB

The crossing out of the second line is presumed to be important, as it's like the fourth line of text, and it may point to some error from the writer. Perhaps the crossed-out "x" above the "o" is important, but who knows? Several cryptographers have attempted to crack the code but to no avail. Most likely, the words are initials of English words but that leaves a lot open for interpretation, as there are quite simply a lot of English words out there.

WRGOABABD (Would Ryan's Grandmother, On A Bicycle, Ascend Backward Downhill?)

I mean, you understand that that's obviously not the answer, but you get the problem here.

The last piece of "evidence" discovered in the book was a phone number, which belonged to a nurse called Jessica Thomson, who lived about 440 yards away from where the body was found. Thomson was interviewed, but she claimed to know nothing about the matter, though she did say that an unknown man had attempted to visit her and had even spoke to a neighbor about her. Thomson was unhappy about her link with the case, but detectives and writers about the case were convinced that she knew more than she let on. Writer Gerry Feltus commented on her evasiveness and desire to avoid talking about the matter.

The Somerton Man or Tamám Shud Case is still being investigated and there are possibilities as to the identity of the person. In 2022, Adelaide University professor Derek Abbott used DNA evidence to identify the man as "Carl Webb," an electrical engineer. The result is still being verified, but police hope that if they can confirm the identity that it may provide a useful new lead about the exact circumstances of the death.

Even with a positive ID on who the man is, however, that doesn't answer the questions about what happened to him. There are several theories, some more plausible than others:

1. He committed suicide, with the words "Tamám Shud" serving as his suicide note. The poem that the words are taken from is all about mortality, however, that doesn't explain why a confirmed cause for death couldn't be found. Is it likely that this man was able to find a way of poisoning himself without leaving any possible trace?

2. The man was a Soviet spy and had been discovered by the Australian secret service and assassinated.

3. The man was a Soviet spy and had turned on Russia, deciding to provide information to Australia instead, which then brought the wrath of the Soviets, who assassinated him.

4. The body had been swapped from the body that eyewitnesses claim they saw the night before, and the *real* Somerton man is long gone.

5. Jessica Thomson knew him and may have been working as a spy herself. Her own daughter claimed that Jessica was adamant that she would never let the information out but was aware of what happened to him.

No possibilities have been fully eradicated or proven. The Somerton man continues to baffle and remains a great mystery of the 20th century. Perhaps if the man's identity is revealed, new links may emerge, and the story can finally be solved. However, one feels that the more time that passes from the day that he was found, the less likely it is that the case will ever fully be solved.

RANDOM EXPLOSION
OR MUTANT SHARKS?

I promise that this one isn't about murder - I truly do. Well, it could *possibly* be about murder, but it's not *definitely* about murder. In fact, it's mainly *likely* that it isn't about murder. Do you see?

Let's stop discussing murder now.

Take yourself back to America in the later quarter of the 19th century, to the 1870s in fact. America had, at this point, been an independent country for a little under a century, had experienced a civil war, and had gone through so many economic booms and collapses that it was hard to keep track. What made the country successful, and wealthy, was its trade. By utilizing their impressive naval trade and exploiting nearby countries and people for their products, the United States became a force to be reckoned with. By 1920, they'd be living lavishly on the profits of war and well on their way to becoming a global superpower (if only it wasn't for that darned Wall St. Crash, eh?).

One such vessel that helped America trade was the *Mary Celeste*, a Canadian-built ship from the 1860s that had been used to trade from the West Indies, up to Nova Scotia, and even across to London. In 1868, the ship had fallen into disrepair under its original name *Amazon*, and it was sold for scrap to a businessman in Nova Scotia, Canada. The ship was restored at great cost, and she became an extremely useful and lucrative ship for traders on the East Coast of America. She continued to have huge amounts of money invested to increase her carrying capacity, new decks were added, and the boat's overall size dramatically increased.

In 1872, the ship's new captain was provided with shares in the boat, as well as command of the vessel that could now carry almost 300 tons. His name was Benjamin Briggs, and he was from Wareham, Massachusetts. Briggs came from a seafaring family, with most of his brothers working at sea, and was a staunch Christian, though he had married his cousin, and I'm genuinely not sure what the New Testament would say about that. Captain Briggs took command of the *Mary Celeste* in October 1872 and was preparing for its first voyage following its huge refit and expansion.

Briggs would be commanding a small crew on a voyage to Genoa, Italy. He chose his crew personally and carefully, going for a mixture of talent and experience for his leadership. The first mate was a well-connected man who had sailed under the captain previously, while the steward came with a personal recommendation from one of the owners of the ship. The four general seamen were Germans who were described as "peaceable and first-class sailors." Essentially, the crew was made up of great sailors who came with high recommendations and buckets of experience. The captain brought his wife and infant daughter with him on the voyage, picturing a peaceful journey with very little that could reasonably go wrong.

So why is it that *Mary Celeste* never made it to Genoa, and the crew were never seen alive again after their departure?

The ship had harbored at New York City for approximately two weeks before its departure on November 5. Captain Briggs oversaw the loading of 1,701 barrels of alcohol and wrote letters to his mother about his confidence in the vessel and the upcoming trip. While waiting for good conditions for their departure date, we should draw attention to a similar ship who was waiting for a cargo of petroleum, which was also going to

Genoa. The ship is called the *Dei Gratia* and was destined for an almost identical route to Italy as the *Mary Celeste*. It was captained by Captain David Morehouse, who set off shortly after the *Mary Celeste* and its small, capable crew.

Fast forward to December 4, and *Dei Gratia* was a short distance from the West Coast of Portugal. Progress had been relatively steady for the captain, and all seemed relatively normal on the waves of the Atlantic Ocean. That is until his helmsman reported that a ship was heading in their direction and appeared unsteady. Upon closer inspection, Morehouse observed that the ship was moving in a bizarre fashion, moving erratically and with its sails set strangely. All concluded that something was wrong with the ship. As they drew nearer, Morehouse saw nobody on deck - where were the crew? Morehouse sent two of his own crew members out on a small boat to board the ship and investigate what was going on.

Morehouse's crew were confident that this was the *Mary Celeste*; they recognized it from when they'd last seen it less than a month before while in New York. Also, it had the words "Mary Celeste" written on it, which was kind of a giveaway.

The men boarded the *Mary Celeste* and found it to be completely deserted. No person, dead or alive, could be found. What they did find didn't immediately explain what had happened either:

- The sails were in poor condition, and some were missing completely.
- The main hatch cover was secure and closed, but others were wide open.
- The single lifeboat was missing.

- The glass housing for the ship's compass (called the binnacle) had smashed.
- There was water up to 3.6 feet in the hold, but this wasn't unusual.
- Someone had made a makeshift sounding rod, an instrument used for measuring the water in the hold, which was abandoned on the deck.

Crucially, the daily log was discovered, which the crew hoped would enlighten them about the situation. The last entry was dated November 25, nine days previously. The position of the *Mary Celeste* was recorded, approximately 400 miles away from where it was found by the *Dei Grata*. Other than this, nothing was noted. No pending disasters or problems were mentioned nor any signs of a struggle. There was a small amount of water in the cabin, and Briggs's cabin had personal items scattered around, including a sword in its sheath. Provisions were ample, all equipment was stowed away appropriately, and the only thing that was missing was the captain's navigational equipment and the ship's papers.

Morehouse decided to bring the *Mary Celeste* into Gibraltar, by dividing his crew into two halves and sailing both boats the 600 miles to the port. Both he and his crew likely expected a hefty payout depending on how salvage hearings went.

This is largely where the evidence of what happened on board the ship ends. Lengthy salvage hearings were carried out, which attempted to ascertain what happened to the crew and whether some disaster had occurred. The hearing was conducted by Frederick Solly-Flood, who most historians agree was essentially quite stupid and had made his mind up before any evidence was presented that a crime had been committed. However, there's not much that insinuates that was the case anyway.

Many theories emerged from the hearing and have been posed by historians since, though (as always) none have been confirmed and so far, the *Mary Celeste* remains a real-life "Ghost Ship":

1. The crew of the *Dei Grata* deliberately scuttled the ship or attacked the crew. This theory proposes that the crew of the *Dei Grata* stood to earn some money upon bringing the ship into Gibraltar, which is true, but they wouldn't have earned much. With a total lack of indication that any violence or aggression occurred, this makes the theory a rather poor one, which is why it was quickly dismissed in the hearing.

2. Theft! Flood was convinced that someone had committed a crime, perhaps some theft. This would seem like a decent theory if it wasn't for the fact that all the alcohol barrels were still on the vessel when it was found. This also rules out piracy, of course.

3. Carrying vast amounts of alcohol can be dangerous. High-proof alcohol is flammable, and perhaps there was a small, pressurized explosion in the hold, which frightened the crew into thinking that the ship was about to explode, so they abandoned it. A decent theory, but there was no sign at all of any sort of explosion or fire.

4. Something natural caused the evacuation. Maybe a huge waterspout or storm caused the crew to panic and leave the ship quickly. This is possible but is only a theory with little evidence to back it up.

5. A huge monster attacked the ship and ate the crew. This is unlikely, but there is a possibility that sharks, or some other sea creature may have attacked the crew. But that would only have happened once they were *already* being in the water...

Unfortunately, there's no answer as to what happened to the crew, but we do know what happened to the ship. In November 1884, a crooked captain crashed the ship into a reef in the hopes of gaining some insurance money.

So at least we know *that* much.

DOES ANYONE HAVE A SHOVEL?

If you've seen the *Pirates of the Caribbean* movies, then your idea of 17th-century pirates is of swashbuckling, handsome types, who fight against corrupt colonizers and for their own twisted form of justice (also gold). This is almost true, except for the fact that many pirates of the time were ravaged by scurvy and other disgusting illnesses due to their lack of hygiene and alcoholism. So be rid of the image of Orlando Bloom climbing the rigging; they were far less Hollywood than that.

Though that may be the case, pirates remain an important part of our world's history. Many of us even forget that pirates were, in fact, real. From the Jolly Rodger flag to the tales of Davey Jones, there truly was a time when working as a sailor in the trade sector or for the government was genuinely dangerous. Infamous names like Blackbeard were spoken with hushed tones and legendary tales emerged about demonically strong buccaneers who couldn't be killed and were sent by the devil.

In truth, though, it was simply lawlessness. In an age without coordinated international security, helicopters, and advanced technology, it was difficult to capture a band of pirates sailing about in the Atlantic Ocean somewhere.

Given all their thieving, murdering, and plundering, some are obsessed with trying to work out where pirates' treasures were buried. There's not always a map where **X** marks the spot, but surely all their "accumulated" wealth must be *somewhere*? Well, this question brings up one of the great mysteries of the 17th and 18th centuries: Where is the treasure of William Kidd?

William Kidd was a Scottish pirate, born in 1654, though details of his childhood and early life are patchy and where there is information, it's uncertain. As a young man, Kidd moved to New York City, which at the time wasn't so filled with hustle and bustle as it is in the 21st century. The East Coast of America was fought over by European settlers, who were desperate to make a bigger claim to the rest of the country (they had no idea how big it was at that point). The English had taken New York City from the Dutch and Kidd settled into life as a popular man, befriending many prominent citizens there, including local governors. We're unsure exactly how Kidd found his sea legs, but we do know that by 1689, he was sailing the seven seas as a pirate.

It's important to know that *privateering* (which is basically piracy) was something that governments were happy to pay sailors to do. Pirates can be very disruptive to other settlements, and as European countries began to grab land in the Caribbean and America, it was handy to have sailors who were willing to give the other "lot" a kick from time to time. By his mid-30s, Kidd was the captain of a ship called the *Blessed William* and had been employed by the Governor of Nevis, an island under English control, to cause some disruption to the French. Kidd led a force to capture £2000, which at the time was a vast sum of money. He'd gained a reputation for reliability and for being a fearsome sailor and pirate.

He continued his pirating antics back in New York City, before setting sail for England in 1695, where he received a commission from the King to do some privateering for his country - to stop the bands of international pirates that made life difficult for the English on the ocean. With the backing of the Crown, Kidd led a feared gang of "pirate-hunters" and set about becoming a respected privateer and a useful tool for England.

Unfortunately, before too long Kidd was essentially working as a pirate himself, taking English ships and vessels from the East India Trading Company (also run by the English). He turned into an enemy of England when he took *Quedagh Merchant*, a colossal, 400-ton ship, in January 1698. Kidd may have thought that he was taking a French ship, as ordered, but it was an Armenian trading vessel and no enemy of the English. Regardless, he took it for himself and went on to capture the *Sedgewick*, which was part of the East India Trading Company's fleet. By March 1698, Kidd was a wanted and hunted man. He was now known as Captain Kidd, one of the great pirate legends, active in the Indian Ocean.

Kidd continued his journey, changing ships and suffering abandonment from his crew who became disgruntled about the lack of money they were receiving. Kidd's pirate fleet disintegrated over time, and he was eventually arrested in Boston, before being executed at Execution Dock for the murder of a sailor and for his continued antics as a pirate. Kidd maintained his innocence but died something of a legend. Stories were written about him, and he was generally well-romanticized.

The big question that comes out of Kidd's story is: What happened to all his treasure?

Before he died in 1701, Kidd was an exceptionally wealthy person. He'd worked hard, stolen a lot, and made sure to gamble well, and as a result, he had a colossal amount of cash. Kidd made sure to carry objects that would be valuable beyond mere money. We know that he possessed thousands of silver and gold bars, many thousands of coins as well as rich textiles and jewels. Some of it, Kidd gave to people, but most of it disappeared.

It's generally accepted that somewhere out there is a vast pirate horde that Captain Kidd hid away from the wider world. Kidd offered up some of his collected wealth upon his arrest, in exchange for his life; he said that he would provide £75,000 worth of treasures, which in modern terms is approximately £8 million. It's generally accepted that Kidd probably had around half a million pounds (in 1700s value) worth of treasures that have yet to be found. Given their age, the gold bars, statues, and jewels would be worth millions upon millions to anyone who finds them in the 21st century.

The baffling thing is that we don't know where the stuff is. It feels almost impossible that after literally hundreds of years of scouring lands that Kidd was known to have spent time in, the treasure hasn't emerged. The largest haul was in 2015, when a 121-pound bar of silver was found off the coast of Madagascar. Most agree that it's likely to be a part of Kidd's treasure, but it's a mere drop in the ocean of how much could be out there. Perhaps the rest is buried underneath a house, hidden in some cave, or even in a random spot on some island somewhere. The fact remains that the greatest pirate treasure is still hidden to this day and remains more elusive than the next *Game of Thrones* book.

THE TWO PRINCES' DISAPPEARANCE

I say Richard, I don't think we're making it to the Coronation!

Being a member of royalty was pretty much one of the only ways to ensure a good life in Medieval England. To say life was difficult for most would be a complete underestimation. With a lack of medical knowledge, dreadful education, and a diet as bland as it still is in 21st-century Britain, it was a painful existence. Royal family members were the only ones who experienced the finer things in life on anything like a regular basis.

Royalty was looked after exceptionally well. They were provided with feasts and total control over the government of England. The great Medieval royals such as William I or Richard I have left everlasting impressions on the landscape of England, by crafting monumental castles and palaces that remain impressive to this day. The monarchs were the ones who commissioned these colossal monuments to power, and the most famous example is one of the oldest, the Tower of London.

The Tower of London was designed by William the First (or William the Conqueror, depending on your outlook on life) who commanded its construction in 1066 when he took the throne of England. Positioned in the center of the City of London, the construction was the tallest building in Europe at the time and could be seen from miles around. Its purpose was to instill fear into the rebellious English population, which William wanted to subjugate and ensure their cooperation.

Over the next few hundred years, the huge castle was transformed and added to. It went from being a royal residence to a prison to a zoo! True story: there are tales of a polar bear residing in the Tower and escaping in order to devour a Londoner or two, a method that the Metropolitan Police Force is considering employing next June.

By the end of the 15th century (1400s, in case you don't know), the Tower was still important to the Crown and especially to Richard III.

The context of this story is important to understand why this bizarre and unsettling tale played out the way it did. In 1483, King Edward IV died quite unexpectedly after falling ill. Edward had two sons, Edward V and Richard of Shrewsbury. English law dictated that Edward would become king and serve like his father before him. However, he was only young at the time and was taken into care with his brother by Richard, their uncle. Richard had the boys put into the Tower of London, the safest building in the country. They couldn't leave, but they had ample space to play, and guards kept a constant watch over their happenings.

While the two young boys, aged 12 and nine, were in the Tower of London, their uncle Richard got to work. Through his connections in the church and popularity among the knights and nobles of the realm, he was able to drum up considerable opposition to the young Prince's claim to the throne. Voices grew louder in powerful circles, proclaiming that the next king should be Richard and not the sons of the late King. With the princes safely locked up, there was little resistance. In fact, the boys barely knew what was going on outside of the Tower - they were fed very little information other than "Your coronation has been postponed" and eventually "Your uncle is now the King, sorry." King Richard III was coronated on July 6, 1483, and the boys remained in the tower.

Herein lies the mystery. There were some reports from Londoners that they'd seen the boys playing on the grounds of the Tower after Richard III's ascension to the throne. We also have notes from a visiting doctor, who said that Prince Edward was stuck with melancholy and seemed to fear for his life. By the end of July 1483, an attempted rescue of the boys had been launched and failed, and no one saw them again. The two princes simply vanished without a trace and without explanation.

I know what you're thinking: They were murdered! And you wouldn't be alone in that assumption; many historians are sure that the princes were murdered and disposed of quickly and quietly. Historians have argued and bickered about *when* the princes died, with some saying that they were alive a year later in July 1484. Others testify that following the failed rescue attempt, they were immediately murdered to put a stop to any potential coup. Unfortunately, we have no evidence whatsoever that proves the boys were murdered. It does seem likely, and movie adaptations from the 1960s paint Richard III as a conniving villain who was happy to murder two young children to secure his kingship. He has the motive, but it also could have been someone else.

Other theories have named Richard III's right-hand man, Henry Stafford, who was executed by the Crown in November 1483. He may have acted on someone else's behalf, or out of selfishness, driven by a hunger to ascend the throne himself as he had a spurious link to the Crown. A few historians have also pointed to Henry VII as the murderer of the princes later, in 1485, as he executed many people who threatened his claim to the throne.

There's also the possibility that the boys weren't murdered at all. Perhaps they escaped the tower or were removed through some European royal link and taken to a safe country to live out their days in comfort. It is also possible that only one died, Edward, as three separate people claimed to be the younger Richard some decades later, which could be true (though is unlikely).

Like everything in this book, however, there is no actual answer to this mystery. Skeletons were found hidden under a staircase in the Tower of London in the 20th century, which led to many assuming that they had been discovered finally. It seemed to answer the question of what happened. Clearly, they had been killed in some gruesome fashion, and their bodies were hidden away, buried in the brickwork of the ancient castle. Unfortunately, the state hasn't allowed any DNA testing to be carried out on the skeletons yet, but they have been buried in Westminster Abbey (where the famous posh ones are buried) in place of the princes.

With no new evidence yet emerging about the goings on at the Tower of London in the late 15th century, it seems likely that there will be no actual conclusion to this story. Whatever happened to the children, it's dreadfully unfortunate. Rumors of their murder spread into mainland Europe quickly and the people of England were quite sure that they'd been quietly disposed of. England was soon to be in the throes of a vicious civil war that would transform the next two centuries of English history, however, the issue of "What happened to the princes?", soon disappeared and was forgotten about. Just another set of dead children, in a time when one out of three children didn't live past the age of five.

IT'S ALL GONE A BIT *BLAIR WITCH*

Shall we have a far more modern mystery, perhaps one that takes place in this century?

The following story occurred in 2018 and is concerned with the world of entertainment. The entertainment industry is a bit mysterious anyway, involving the otherworldly talents and beauties of movies and music. For many, it's a world that entices and excites. However, it's also beset by strange stories and tragedies. We can all think of cases of actors being driven to drink and drugs to keep up with the pressures of fame, or horrific injuries or illnesses that came from a project designed to bring a smile to people's faces.

We're focusing on a man called Terrence Woods Jr, who was 26 in 2018 and had just returned from a long trip abroad. An American man who lived in Maryland, he'd taken off to see the world as a young person and to experience more of what life had to offer. On his return, he was employed as a production assistant and was working for the Discovery Channel. You know - the channel that will screen a David Attenborough documentary one minute and *SHARK WEEK: THERE WILL BE BLOOD* the next.

Woods was working on a documentary entitled *Gold Rush: Dave Turin's Lost Mine* as part of a 12-person crew. Production assistants, for those that don't know, do a lot to aid the production of television shows including but not limited to preparing the lights, ensuring props are set, assisting costume designers, and printing paperwork - basically, they do all the stuff that others think they're too important to do. Many great directors and producers start as production assistants and work their way up. No doubt Woods saw that career path laid out in front of him.

The crew were following the host: Dave Turin, as he explored abandoned mines in the mountainous regions of the Western United States. They'd arrived in Idaho on October 5, 2018, and Woods commemorated the occasion with an Instagram post, a photo of a densely packed forest with the caption "Idaho." It was to be his last Instagram post.

With filming packing up, Woods told a woman from the local area who had been assisting the production, mainly with transport, that he was going to the bathroom. Before anyone could enquire as to whether it was a number one or two, he'd turned around and was walking away. The associate producer quickly observed that Woods had dropped his radio to the floor; not advisable, especially in the remote forest regions that they were filming in. Tragedies happen in such places, and the producer became instantly concerned for Woods's safety.

Woods suddenly broke off into a run, careering down a steep cliff that led into the dense forest. He disappeared into the thicket and the crew tore after him. Later, the associate producer would tell news reporters that he'd never seen someone run so fast before, which was doubly strange considering the dangerous terrain. The crew members lost Woods quickly and many of them injured themselves within moments of attempting to descend the cliff face. They returned to the site of the shoot with several rips in their clothing and blood streaking their outfits.

That was the last that anyone saw of Terrence Woods Jr; he'd simply vanished. The crew, who were employed by *RAW TV*, phoned in a 911 call at about half past six, reporting the young man as missing. In the call, the employee detailed that Woods had had a breakdown earlier that day and was clearly struggling with his mental health, as if providing some sort of reason for his disappearance. However, when probed for more detail on this, the employee retracted the comment, and Woods's mental state wasn't called into question again. Given the fact that it was dark, the sheriff's department decided to begin searching the following morning for Woods. With a full team scouring the forest near where Woods had disappeared, alongside sniffer dogs and high-tech heat detection equipment, they turned up no evidence of where the man had vanished.

After about a week, the police called off the search and had nothing to report back. Terrence Woods Jr had simply gone away without so much as a trace, tearing off into the forest at breakneck speed for a reason that seemed to evade everyone on shoot.

The whole mystery deepened over the coming months. Very public campaigns were run on social media and *FOX 5* curated a podcast episode of *Missing Pieces* where they attempted to answer questions related to Woods's disappearance. The podcast producers tried several times to get in contact with any crew that was present when Woods was working there, but none of them would talk. The podcast secured an interview with one of the locals who helped organize some transport and local knowledge, but the crew was tight-lipped.

Before long, Terrence's parents went public with some of their suspicions. His mother, Valerie, asserted that Terrence was a responsible young man and there was no good reason, that she could think of, as to why he would have run off so immediately unless threatened. Valerie and her husband, Terrence Woods Sr, claim that they think their son was mistreated by the *RAW TV* production and may have been the victim of racism or intimidation from members of the crew.

RAW TV claims that they have been completely transparent in the search for Terrence Woods Jr and that there's been no hiding of any information whatsoever. The police have investigated thoroughly, and the case remains open. They found no evidence that the crew of the documentary had been abusive or intimidating to the young man. Bizarrely, when the parents met the associate producer, who was the last person to see Terrence Woods Jr, he hastened to tell them how bad Terrence was at his job. The associate producer was quick to mention that he felt Terrence questioned basic instructions and wasn't going to be around for the long term in the business. Which is both a weird thing to say and suspicious, or at least, that's how Terrence's parents felt.

Unfortunately, Woods is still a missing person, and the case continues to baffle law enforcement. The dense forests of Western America are dangerous, and it is easy for people to become lost or disoriented while exploring them. If Woods suffered a mental breakdown and sprinted into the distance, it would have been easy for him to fail to find his way home.

The biggest mystery of all is how law enforcement hasn't found any evidence to reach a conclusion on the case. How does a person simply disappear like that? There've been no good leads on his whereabouts, his clothes haven't been found, no body has been discovered over the years, and he hasn't attempted to pass through international borders.

For now, Terrence Woods Jr is a missing person. No one knows why he ran off like he did, and no one seems to know what's happened to him since, but his friends and family continue to hold out hope that he might be discovered soon.

"I SWEAR, I LEFT THEM RIGHT HERE!"

- Three Years Later -

Colonization. A word that today strikes up many ill feelings and for good reason. Colonization, if you're not sure what it is, is the act of taking a place (and often its people) for one's own use. Famously many parts of the world were colonized from the 15th century and well into the 19th century by White Europeans, who discovered land and resources, plus used modern technologies to overwhelm, subjugate, and destroy indigenous populations. Most infamously this happened across America, Africa, and Australia.

America received a great deal of attention from European countries when it was "discovered" in the late 15th century. States vied for land on the continent, particularly the East Coast. Initially, it wasn't realized just how important the land of America could be, but as its vast size was understood better, and the resources began to be tallied, colonization sped up. The Indigenous Americans were treated harshly by the colonizers, who would often rely on lying to the people or using acts of violence to get their way. By the end of the 16th century, England had their eyes on America and made their first attempts to create English colonies there.

Sir Walter Raleigh, one of England's most notable statesmen during Elizabeth I's reign, drew up the plans for England's first colony in the "New World." He chose a small island in what is now Dare County, North Carolina. Raleigh had previously sent out two ships, telling the captains to identify any areas worth colonizing in the region. The two captains came back with a unanimous vote: Roanoke. The sailors reported that the local indigenous Americans were very hospitable and had met Europeans before. As a result, there was no hostility and relations seemed like they'd be easily forged. Beyond this, Roanoke was well-positioned strategically, both regarding trade and any naval military involvement. The reports described the area as both pleasant and bountiful, even drawing comparisons to the Garden of Eden, though most historians and any residents of Dare County will agree that this was Walter Raleigh talking out of his backside (I'm only joking, please don't send any hate mail).

The point is that the decision was made. Roanoke would be the site of the very first English colony in America, and it was an exciting moment for Elizabethan England, which had grown strong under the Queen's leadership. Raleigh made his preparations and sent a fleet of seven ships to the new land with Sir Richard Grenville leading the expedition. Ralph Lane was appointed the governor of the new colony and would oversee the expedition ensuring its long-lasting survival. Some 600 men all in all were sent to Roanoke, with the idea that half of them would stay there and set up the new society.

The fleet reached Roanoke in May 1585; however, only two of the boats made it and lots of provisions were lost en route, which meant that the colony was simply not going to be able to support some 300 people. Grenville decided that a little over 100 would stay with Lane, which would be enough for now, as a second fleet was due to leave in June 1585.

This first colony was an unmitigated disaster, with the colonizers failing to sustain adequate crop supplies for themselves. They leaned on the local indigenous Americans for food, who became frustrated by the Europeans' lack of fortitude and the disease that they seemed to bring with them. The "Lane Colony" collapsed in

1586, but England was confident that Roanoke *could* work. So, it established another governor in John White and provided another 100 settlers, and the colony was resettled in 1587.

White helped get things going for the colony, but things were looking tough. The colonizers decided to move some 50 miles away from the original site where they hoped crops would grow better and they wouldn't be so associated with the previous site in the eyes of the indigenous Americans. The people told White that things weren't looking good and that they needed supplies from England. He reluctantly agreed to return to England with a small fleet, so that they may return quickly with supplies. White left the colonizers on August 27, 1587.

White tried desperately to get back to the colony, which he knew needed help, but England's war with the Spanish was hotting up. White was told, in no uncertain terms, that he wouldn't be returning to the colony but would instead need to fight the Spanish in naval battles. It took White three years to return to Roanoke, reaching the colony in August of 1590. When he arrived, there were no colonizers left. In fact, there was no sign of any European life whatsoever, and there were no corpses; they had all vanished.

White had left his wife and daughter with the colony and desperately searched for signs of the 110+ people that had once resided there. There were few clues, if any at all, apart from one word carved into a post…

CROATOAN

Croatoan was the name of the island, which was the home to a group of indigenous Americans who went by the same name. The obvious answer is the one that was assumed by the preceding investigations into the colony's demise: The people had been annihilated by the Croatoans, and none had been left alive. There weren't signs of a struggle or conflict, however, and it seemed unlikely that the colonizers would have simply walked off to their doom. Unfortunately, the first crew were unable to stay long to investigate. A storm had rushed in, and they had to turn back to England almost immediately to escape it.

The other possibility is that the colonizers had moved somewhere. Perhaps they'd sought a better spot inland, or up the coast, or perhaps they had simply moved to Croatoan Island and settled into life with the indigenous Americans. This seems less likely, however - DNA tests in the late 20th century gave no indication that there had been any kind of assimilation from Europeans into the Croatoan people.

Other historians have supposed that the colony became intimidated at the task ahead or were overwhelmed by hostility from the indigenous Americans and difficult conditions. Possessing boats, they may have then attempted to sail back to England but failed in their journey. Their boat could have been lost in a storm or scuttled somewhere remote. They may have come into conflict with the Spanish, who would have happily taken their ships given the war unfolding at the time. The problem with this theory is that, likely, the Spanish would have bragged about such a haul and may have taken credit for thwarting the attempted English colonization.

The Roanoke mystery has very little chance of being solved, now about 450 years on from the event itself. All answers are very possible but just don't have enough evidence to support them as the definitive solution. I'm surprised that no one has considered a team of Bigfoot yet as the answer, but I hold out hope for some evidence soon.

HELP! I'VE KNOCKED HIS HEAD OFF!

If you've ever read or seen the *Harry Potter* series, then you might be aware of the magical prison Azkaban. The (supposedly) inescapable prison for evil wizards is located on a small island, surrounded by harsh waters, and guarded by brutal guards. Though the bespeckled boy fighting against the forces of evil while attempting to get off with his best friend's sister is made up, the prison in *Harry Potter* is based on a real prison: Alcatraz.

Alcatraz is an island, which used to operate as a military base until it was officially turned into a prison in 1934. America had experienced a serious crime wave throughout the 1920s and 30s, and the Department of Justice thought that an unescapable prison would help curb the rising levels of criminality. Positioned about a mile and a half off the coast of San Francisco, it's impossible to get away from the island without a good boat, a helicopter, or wings, hence why pigeons aren't imprisoned there. The water is bone-chillingly cold and attempting to swim through it would result in death; no human would be able to survive the attempt.

Over time, Alcatraz earned a reputation as one of the toughest prisons in the US, which is saying something as the nation takes its "prisoning" quite seriously. Prisoners who came out of Alcatraz repeatedly reported that they were treated brutally, with guards physically and mentally harming the prisoners. Beyond this, the conditions of the building were described as inhumane. It was never designed to hold prisoners for long periods; it was meant to be a fort for defense purposes. As such, the effects of the place on all who were held there were serious.

Suicide became associated with Alcatraz quickly. The first suicide was carried out in 1937 and was in no way the last.

Criticism of Alcatraz accompanied it since its inception as a prison, with writers claiming that it failed in its most basic aims. It seemed that Alcatraz was there to test the prisoners and to push them to their limits, rather than offering some path to rehabilitation. Alcatraz was inescapable and unlivable, a true hell-on-Earth scenario.

So, if you found yourself imprisoned there, you might as well *try* and escape, right?

Alcatraz saw its fair share of attempted escapes, but they mostly just didn't work. Even if you managed to slip past the dozens of guards and get over the outer walls, you had to contend with a mile and a half of ice-cold water. Thirty-six prisoners attempted to escape Alcatraz, with 23 of them being caught in the act. A further six were shot in the process and two drowned. There *were* three, however, who may have made it. The penitentiary is sure that they died in their escape attempt, but others say that they successfully escaped the prison from hell.

Their names were Frank Morris, John Anglin, and Clarence Anglin. Frank was in for armed robbery and prison escape. Brothers John and Clarence attempted bank robberies together as well. A fourth man, Allen West, was involved in the planning. He had been imprisoned for car theft and had an impressive arrest record (more than 20!). Essentially, these guys were great at thieving, just not the "getting away with it" part, which is arguably the most important bit.

The four criminals were literally as "thick as thieves," in that they all knew each other and got on well before they spent time in Alcatraz. They'd met at prisons in Florida and Georgia. When they were assigned adjacent cells upon their incarceration in 1961, they began formulating a foolproof plot to escape Alcatraz. It does feel like a clerical error to place them so close to each other. Perhaps someone with a brain could have looked at their histories and not put them together, but hey-ho.

Frank Morris was the leader of the crew, very much the Top Cat of this gang. For six months, they worked on widening the ventilation ducts underneath their sink, which would help them get out of their cells whenever they wanted. Taking care to work during "music hour" and using Morris's accordion for cover, they beavered away with metal spoons and saw type blades that they'd found about the prison. Clearly, inspections weren't very stringent at Alcatraz in the 1960s...

Once out of their cells, they had access to a utility corridor running behind them. Morris determined that the vacant area that was the top level of the cellblock would be a perfect location for them to set up a workshop, to make some real preparations for their eventual escape. Morris's first port of call was to create life preservers, which might allow them to battle the waters outside of Alcatraz. The team collected about 50 raincoats and then created life preservers, using an article from a magazine that Morris had been given in prison. Imagine that. They decided to give criminals who have a history of escaping prison, a guide on how to make life preservers, thus nullifying the only method that the Department of Justice has to keep them in. Amazing!

The prison also had an overabundance of liquid plastic in their workshops, which was pilfered by the crew and used to construct a raft that measured 6 x 14 feet. Using bits of plywood to construct pallets, they only had to remove the industrial fan that obstructed their way out to the roof, and it seemed that the gang was ready to make their attempt.

The most important element, beyond the boat, was to ensure that the four men had time. Time to build the raft and life preservers, and time to escape the dreaded prison. To buy themselves this precious time, they built diversions similar to how Ferris Bueller tricked his parents into thinking he was at school in the 1986 movie. Through some ingenious arts and crafts, the men made fake heads that looked *a bit* like themselves. By using toothpaste, soap, concrete dust, and toilet paper, they were able to mold a paper-mâché type material, onto which they popped some hair from the hairdressers. Once they'd stuffed blankets and pillows under their covers, the subterfuge was convincing enough that a passing warden would simply think that they were having a slow morning getting up.

They had a diversion, they had a way out of the prison, and they had a way off the island. They were ready.

The foursome launched their plan on June 11, 1962. It started with an immediate problem: Allen West's cement had hardened in his cell, which meant he couldn't climb out into the tunnel. Well, being the loyal men they were, the brothers and Frank Morris thought for a few seconds about how they could help West..., before deciding to leave him behind and escape themselves. West went back to bed and cursed the cement gods for preventing him from freedom.

Climbing out into the service corridor, through a ventilation shaft, and onto the roof, the prisoners let out a huge crash of metal as they appeared on the rooftop. Guards heard this but for some reason decided it wasn't worth investigating, leaving the three men counting their blessings, as well as counting their live preservers. After descending the 50-foot walls and climbing over dangerous 12-foot barbed-wire fences, the men located a blind spot in the guard's vision. Around 10.00 p.m. they aimed their boat at Angel Island and set off!

The morning bell rang through the prison on June 12 for the inmates to rise from their beds for breakfast, but three cells in Cell Block B remained undisturbed as the prisoners shuffled toward the canteen. Allen West was likely feverishly checking over his shoulder to see if his co-conspirators would drift out for breakfast like the rest of the inmates, but there was no sign of them. If this were a movie, then he'd give a wry smile and say something like, "You dogs." However, this isn't a movie, and West was probably very angry that they'd succeeded without him, so he may have just sworn repeatedly. Meanwhile, Alcatraz's exceptionally well-trained guards laughed to each other about the lazy, sleepy prisoners and left them alone in their beds. If they didn't want breakfast, so be it.

After a few hours, the guards had had enough and one reached into the cell of Frank Morris, pushing his head, telling him to get up. The guard then stood with his mouth agape, like a monkey staring at his own reflection, as Frank's head rolled off the bed and onto the floor! The guard gathered himself for a second, understanding that he hadn't just brutally murdered a prisoner, and realized the head was fake. The alarm was instantly sounded, and the guards rushed into the two cells of the Anglin brothers. Empty.

As a thorough sweep of the prison was conducted, the FBI arrived at Alcatraz. They found the widened air ducts that led into a service tunnel, where they found the men's tools. The investigators then located the open vent in the ceiling of the tunnel, through which the men had clambered onto the roof. From the roof, they figured they'd jumped the fence and set off.

The FBI was confident that the men had died in the icy waters off the shore of Alcatraz, as others had done before them. However, no bodies were found, and the life raft wasn't discovered either. Approximately a month after the escape, a Norwegian ship saw a body floating in the water, which the authorities were confident would have been one of the men. However, the San Francisco County Coroner, Henry Turkel, was quick to point out that bodies don't float endlessly, and it's unlikely that one of the prisoners would be bobbing about in the water a month after his death.

The raft and the prisoners haven't been located to this day. Frank, John, and Clarence are all still on the FBI Most Wanted list, and the authorities receive calls from time to time, claiming to have information. All the calls and investigations have led to nothing.

The big question is: What happened after they escaped? Here are a few possibilities:

1. They died. We must consider the idea that the FBI are correct in their assumption that the three prisoners simply died. Extensive searches were carried out by land, sea, and air, and nothing conclusive turned up to provide evidence of the prisoner's successful trip. Of course, nothing had turned up to say it was unsuccessful, either.

2. The men lived out the rest of their days in San Francisco, or somewhere else in America. FBI investigations said that it's possible they stole a car and managed to forge identity documents somewhere down the line. In the years after their escape, the FBI received a litany of phone calls and messages saying that the prisoners had been spotted, but all leads came to a dead end. If the men did this, they've done it *very* well.

3. The men had escaped to Mexico. They could have driven there, and with slacker border control in the 1960s compared to today, crossing over wouldn't have been impossible. In fact, an Alcatraz inmate called Thomas Kent claimed in an interview in 1993, that he had helped to plan the escape. He said that Clarence Anglin's girlfriend was to pick the trio up and drive them all to Mexico immediately. Most don't believe this, however, as the man was paid a decent fee for his interview, and he probably lied so that he could secure it.

No one knows, of course. But the escape was extremely famous. In 1963, the author J. Campbell Bruce wrote a book documenting the escape called *Escape from Alcatraz*, and a film of the same name was later produced. You're welcome to consider any ending for the story that you like. The case is officially closed with no answer.

THE HOUSING ASSOCIATION FROM HELL

Bruce Willis
is a ghost
the whole time

This story has been covered, with some embellishments, by Netflix in a movie titled *The Watcher*, so if it piques your interest (and it's not 2040 when Netflix is irrelevant), feel free to go and learn a bit more. Of course, if you've already watched the Netflix movie, then feel free to feel disappointed that this chapter may now be something of a damp squib for you, close the book, and eat a chocolate bar.

This case is an eerie one and sounds like something from a horror movie, hence why Netflix decided to turn it into a true crime documentary. It attacks our sensibilities and understanding that suburban America is a safe place, utilizing the same horror that made *Halloween* so scary way back in 1979.

We start our story in June 2014, when a couple by the name of Maria and Derek Broaddus were preparing to move into their new home with their three children. The address was 657 Boulevard in Westfield, New Jersey, and it was well located in the "30th Safest City in the US."

Maria and Derek had barely completed the sale of the property, mere days had passed in fact, when they received a letter addressed to:

The New Owner

This could have been anything; a marketing letter from some anonymous company, or something to do with the local housing association. Unfortunately, it seemed to be neither. The letter's contents were disturbing.

The first paragraph was odd, but not necessarily threatening:

"Dearest new neighbor of 657 Boulevard, allow me to welcome you to the neighborhood … Did 657 Boulevard call to you with its force within? 657 Boulevard has been the subject of my family for decades now, and as it approaches its 110th birthday, I have been put in charge of watching and waiting for its second coming. My grandfather watched the house in the 1920s and my father watched it in the 1960s. It is now my time."

Very, very strange. The writer alludes to some sort of power or force within the property, which has required the careful "watching" of members of their family over the years. Maria and Derek were perplexed, which soon gave way to horror as they read on:

"…There are hundreds and hundreds of cars that drive by 657 Boulevard each day. Maybe I am in one. Look at all the windows you can see…maybe I am in one. Look out any of the many windows in 657 Boulevard at all the people who stroll by each day. Maybe I am one…You have children. I have seen them. So far, I think there are three that I have counted…Do you need to fill the house with the young blood I requested? Better for me. Was your old house too small for the growing family? Or was it greed to bring me your children? Once I know their names I will call to them and draw them to me."

It's the sort of anonymous correspondence that would turn any parent's blood cold with fear. This "Watcher," as they had signed the letter, was making oblique threats to their children's safety and seemed to have some sort of knowledge about the local area and their family!

The Broaddus couple reached out to the previous owners who had lived there for 23 years. John and Andrea Woods admitted

135

that they had once received a letter from "the Watcher," but only one. With that in mind, the Broaddus family decided that it was probably some local oddball and if they'd not bothered the Woods family, it was unlikely that they'd bother the Broaddus family. The letter was discarded - out of sight, out of mind.

After two weeks, the family hadn't yet fully moved in, and the Watcher made contact again. This time, the children's nicknames were referred to, and specific details of the house were included.

> "Will the young blood play in the basement? Or are they too afraid to go down there alone. I would [be] very afraid if I were them. It is far away from the rest of the house. If you were upstairs you would never hear them scream…will you all sleep on the second floor? Who has the bedrooms facing the street? I'll know as soon as you move in."

Maria and Derek fully halted the move at this point. The Watcher sent another letter, which simply read:

> "Where have you gone to? 657 Boulevard is missing you."

The Broadduses contacted the police who returned no information on who this person was. Harassed and seemingly stalked by an unknown figure, Maria's and Derek's mental health suffered drastically. They'd put their life savings into this house, after all. The couple attempted to sue the Woods family, who had lived in the house previously, for failing to disclose their sole contact with the Watcher, but the judge threw the case out.

The Broadduses then spoke with a developer about splitting the housing plot into two, which might disrupt the Watcher or possibly stop them altogether, considering there'd be two houses with different addresses. If this plan came to fruition, 657 Boulevard would be eradicated from existence. Local neighborhood planning boards objected, however, and families appealed against the Broadduses attempts to split the property, indicating that the two plots would be too small. However, it's interesting to note that that same board would later allow a similar-sized plot (actually, a bit smaller) to split in two.

Somehow, despite the media attention that the house had garnered, the Broaddus family was able to rent out their home on the strict condition that a threatening letter arriving would end the rental agreement instantly. It didn't take long for the Watcher to get back in touch:

> *"To The vile and spiteful Derek and his wench of a wife Maria.*

> *657 Boulevard survived your attempted assault and stood strong...My soldiers of the Boulevard followed my orders to a T. They carried out their mission and saved the soul of 657 Boulevard with my orders. All hail The Watcher!!!...Maybe a car accident. Maybe a fire. Maybe something as simple as a mild illness that never seems to go away but makes you fall sick day after day after day after day after day. Maybe the mysterious death of a pet. Loved ones suddenly die. Planes and cars and bicycles crash. Bones break. You are despised by the house...and The Watcher won."*

For some reason, the tenants agreed to stay in the property after receiving this letter but had cameras installed.

The case was turned into a horror movie in 2016, despite several attempts by Derek and Maria to stop it, including a cease-and-desist order. In 2019, they managed to sell the house at a

$400,000 loss. The new owners haven't reported any letters from the Watcher, and the trail has gone cold, with no arrests and no conclusive evidence as to who it could be.

So, what are the theories?

1. It's the Broadduses! The Scooby-Doo guess would be the Broadduses themselves. Perhaps suffering from buyer's remorse or even seeking a movie deal further down the line, the couple could have forged the whole thing to create this creepy scenario. What makes the theory less strong is that the Broadduses suffered genuine psychological trauma because of the event, verified by their doctor. Beyond this, the Woods family had received a letter before them and, it turns out, so had another family living in a different house.

2. Michael Langford, it's always Michael Langford! Langford was a neighbor of the Broaddus family and lived next door to 657 Boulevard with his 90-year-old mother. He was known as a local oddball, who liked to spook his neighbors by looking into their windows and backyards. DNA testing was performed on the Langford family, as some DNA had been found on the letters, but there was no match at all. The Langfords were dropped as suspects almost immediately, and the Broaddus family felt that this was odd.

3. It was "The Gamer." There's an anonymous suspect simply called "The Gamer" who liked to play online video games under the alias "The Watcher." He had a penchant for quite violent and disturbing games and agreed to be interviewed by the police to clear his (unknown) name.

However, he never showed up to the interviews, and the police didn't have enough evidence to maintain him as a suspect.

The Watcher case appears to have gone cold now, with the letters having stopped and the current tenants living a quite normal life. However, it remains peculiar that no one was even arrested in relation to the letters. No physical altercation or online trail has rendered it a difficult case to investigate. It's likely that The Watcher still lives in the area and could do it all again.

CONCLUSION

And so, concludes our compendium of mysteries. In this book, I've tried to bring you some genuinely baffling cases that aren't yet solved and don't look like they're going to be.

This is partially for your enjoyment, and partially so the book may be reprinted in later years and remain relevant. Clever, right?

There are undoubtedly many mysteries that don't feature in this book that *could* feature in it. You might have expected the Bermuda Triangle to be included, but there are many good theories as to what happens there, and most of the stories are fabricated anyway.

Without a doubt, there's more mystery out there to discover, which is a good thing.

Our lives are so often without any mystery at all. We go to our jobs, we go home, we go to the gym - some of us might even work out there sometimes!

But most of what we do is comfortable, and we know everything about it. It's good to know that there is a mystery in this world, and we have to come to terms with the fact that we simply don't know everything, and for the stories in this book - we never will know everything.

Hopefully, you've enjoyed this book immensely and want to tell all of your friends and family about it. This collection has been carefully curated to be as original as possible and to provide great historical knowledge at the same time as being genuinely interesting - so don't be shy about spreading the word!

I hope that you've learned a few things about our human history and have been captivated by the odd tales within.

And just remember, if you receive an anonymous letter addressed to "the owner of _____," make sure you secure a Netflix deal before you open it. It could make you a millionaire!

www.ingramcontent.com/pod-product-compliance
Lightning Source LLC
Chambersburg PA
CBHW071213020426
42333CB00015B/1395